SHORT CUTS

INTRODUCTIONS TO FILM STUDIES

OTHER TITLES IN THE SHORT CUTS SERIES

THE HORROR GENRE: FROM BEELZEBUB TO BLAIR WITCH
Paul Wells

THE STAR SYSTEM: HOLLYWOOD'S PRODUCTION OF POPULAR IDENTITIES
Paul McDonald

SCIENCE FICTION CINEMA: FROM OUTERSPACE TO CYBERSPACE
Geoff King and Tanya Krzywinska

EARLY SOVIET CINEMA: INNOVATION, IDEOLOGY AND PROPAGANDA
David Gillespie

DISASTER MOVIES: THE CINEMA OF CATASTROPHE
Stephen Keane

THE WESTERN GENRE: FROM LORDSBURG TO BIG WHISKEY
John Saunders

NEW CHINESE CINEMA: CHALLENGING REPRESENTATIONS
Sheila Cornelius

READING HOLLYWOOD

SPACES AND MEANINGS IN AMERICAN FILM

DEBORAH THOMAS

WALLFLOWER

LONDON and NEW YORK

A Wallflower Paperback

First published in Great Britain in 2001 by Wallflower Press
16 Chalk Farm Road, Camden Lock, London NW1 8AG
www.wallflowerpress.co.uk

A catalogue record for this book is available from the British Library

ISBN 1 903364 01 9

Book Design by Rob Bowden Design

Printed in Great Britain by Creative Print and Design Group, (Wales) Ltd.

For the family I came from: Rae, Sidney and David Thomas, and David Ellis

CONTENTS

LIST OF ILLUSTRATIONS

ACKNOWLEDGEMENTS

I am grateful to more friends, colleagues and students than I can adequately single out here, not only for general support for this project, but for so many conversations – in the classroom, at conferences, at work and elsewhere, both electronically and in person – where my perplexities and enthusiasms were given space to express themselves and received thoughtful responses and encouraging words.

I would like to give specific mention to Douglas Pye for generously sharing his ideas and commenting on some of mine, and for pointing me towards Fritz Lang's *Cloak and Dagger* with its mirror shots of offscreen space. Thanks, as well, to Victor Perkins for making it possible for me to see *Party Girl* and *Advise and Consent* in their original formats, and to Susan Smith and Lee Barron for their recommendations of several books from which I have drawn.

I would also like to mention the splendid conference on *Style and Meaning* held at the University of Reading in March 2000 and, more particularly, the workshop offered by Douglas Pye and John Gibbs on *Bonjour Tristesse* which reinforced my own hope that Preminger be put back on the Film Studies agenda again, a hope that motivated my close look at *Advise and Consent* in the present book.

For technical help and advice, offered with patience and good humour, heartfelt thanks to Phil Biggs and Irfan Ul Haq at the University of Sunderland. I am also grateful to Yoram Allon, my editor at Wallflower Press, with whom it has been such a pleasure to work.

Finally, as ever, I thank John Smith and our daughter Natasha, who cheer me up and calm me down.

INTRODUCTION

This is not a 'how-to' book, as if reading films were a mechanical process that could be achieved by following a preconceived set of rules in order to arrive at a fixed and uniform result. To read a film is to engage with it in all of its detail as a starting point for talking about things that matter and, in the process, to discover the common ground between the film and us, in some cases in spite of a considerable passage of time between the film's initial appearance and our subsequent reading.

In the words of Stanley Cavell, a reading is 'a term I use in part to suggest that the next time I speak about the subject it will probably go differently' (1996: xi). However, although a given film may provide a concrete basis for focusing our concerns and assisting us in following a particular train of thought, this is not to imply that the resultant readings develop a life of their own independent of the film's particularities and are wholly a matter of subjective response. Neither need such readings necessarily match up with the intentions of the film-makers who produced the films in the first place. They can most usefully be understood as sustained meditations grounded in the detailed specifics of their texts. At their best, such accounts invite those to whom they are offered to revisit the films and see for themselves, enriching their own experiences with new depth and bringing significant details to their attention in fresh and productive ways, while ultimately encouraging such viewers to make up their own minds as to how true to their own experiences of the film the readings may be, and how illuminating and important the issues that they raise.

Not all films are up to close scrutiny, of course, with some much more bountiful in the opportunities for thought which they offer than others. While some may be thin and merely formulaic, others appear almost inexhaustible as objects of reflection and discovery, sustaining readings and re-readings from many perspectives and along many lines. In this book I hope to suggest a number of useful questions we can ask about significant spaces in American films and the related thematic preoccupations they open up by primarily, but not exclusively, concentrating on films from the period when the studio system was dominant. Each of the four chapters will thus place its main emphasis upon a different aspect of this approach.

In Chapter 1, my starting point will be the settings of John Ford's *My Darling Clementine* (1946) and Nicholas Ray's *Party Girl* (1958), ranging from broad geographical locations and features, through to architectural structures and their layouts, and unobtrusive details in a scene's decor. In contrast, Chapter 2 will emphasise what I shall be referring to as dramaturgical spaces, particularly private and public spaces and the traffic between them. Here I shall concentrate on a number of small-town family melodramas whose concerns with scandal tend to identify the private arena with the family home and the public arena with the small town as a whole. Nevertheless, no physical space is inherently private or public, since the identification of a space with either one of these depends on the sort of dramas which take place within them and the nature of the access to them which other characters are given. Thus, dramaturgical space refers to something distinct from the specific physical spaces discussed in Chapter 1. In Chapter 3 I shall focus on cinematic aspects of space which, unlike settings, are inaccessible to the characters but depend upon the nature of the film as a film. The ways that editing and camera movement shape our knowledge of the spaces of the narrative world – and our attitudes to the characters and events within them – will be examined with reference to a single film, Otto Preminger's *Advise and Consent*. Finally, in Chapter 4, I will look at the space we occupy as spectators and the relationship between this and the spaces within the films themselves. Rather than seeing such spaces as unproblematically distinct – with characters firmly located within their narrative worlds and us equally firmly located outside them – I shall pay particular attention to the ambiguities and potential breakdowns in such a schema. In all four chapters, however, the initial concentration on a particular aspect of space is intended as a springboard to many other issues. In particular, I am interested in where such thoughts about space may lead us: we need a way of kick-starting our reading – a workable response to the question 'Where do we begin?' when faced with a film – and questions about space are as good a route into the films as any other.

An example or two before we launch ourselves into the discussion proper may be useful to clarify some of the things I mean by 'meaning'. For instance, in Frank Capra's *It's a Wonderful Life* (1946), there is a moving scene when Peter Bailey (Samuel S. Hinds) is talking with his son George (James Stewart) at the dining room table, expressing his wish that George will come back to work at the Bailey Building and Loan Company on his return from college in four years' time, and George is uneasily attempting to explain his reluctance to do so without appearing to criticise his father after the latter's years of self-sacrifice for the sake of the company. The subtleties of the two actors' performances are worthy of our attention and make it difficult to detach ourselves sufficiently from the emotional focus of the scene to look around at the details of the domestic setting. However, if we manage to do so, we may notice two cases of mounted butterflies in frames on the wall in the background behind Peter Bailey. It may be presumed that the butterflies have been collected by George, since they make an appearance later in his marital home, a repetition which reinforces the sense of their importance, and one of their functions in the scene with George and his father is undoubtedly to enhance the homeliness of the setting and to indicate the pride that George's parents feel towards their sons. Nevertheless, in a film about an angel trying to earn his wings and one in which George himself longs to travel and is continually frustrated in his desires – while having to show pride and conceal resentment at his younger brother's wartime su cess as a flier – it is certainly pertinent that the objects on the wall are butterflies rather than anything else.

FIGURE 1 *Butterflies*

Furthermore, what we have on the wall are not paintings of butterflies in flight, but actual butterflies immobilised and dead. As such, they relate to the travel posters which George's wife Mary (Donna Reed) puts up in an old house on their honeymoon night as a well-meant, but inadvertently mocking, substitute for any real fulfilment of his dreams to spread his wings. However, the fact that the butterflies are visually linked to George's father more than to George himself through the composition of the image which places the butterflies at Peter Bailey's back is also important. So too is the way that George's father increasingly reveals his own disappointment through the scene, encouraging George to do all he can to get away from Bedford Falls and realise his ambitions, rather than remaining and crawling to Potter (Lionel Barrymore) as he himself has had to do. The scene is George's – and our – last view of his father, since he is to die offscreen later that night when George is at his brother's high school graduation celebrations, and George's decision to attend the graduation party is a direct result of his unease and embarrassment as his father's sense of failure reveals itself while they talk.

In writing these few words about the scene, I find that there is so much more to say and think about than I have room to offer here. This one small detail in the film's decor serves to unlock a number of issues relating to other scenes and characters than the ones at hand, while ranging over a number of important themes: freedom, filial duty, disappointment, and so on, as well as the specific form such preoccupations take for men in the post-war American small town and the way values are passed on from father to son. Regardless of whether we wish to say that the butterflies 'mean' or 'symbolise' anything specific, they clearly do resonate, suggesting and helping us to remain aware of key aspects of the film's thematic concerns by integrating such issues into the setting itself. The film's meanings are thus not so much a set of propositions which can be readily detached from the film but rather a complex combination of themes and their simultaneous embodiments in a number of elements: the film's sound and look, its details of performance and camera rhetoric, its structure and tone. Thus, the meanings are embedded in the texture of the film itself. Film criticism can prise such details away from the whole through the explicitness of its linguistic descriptions, thereby bringing them and some of the issues they open up to our attention. However, no such account is likely to be an adequate substitute for apprehending the complexity of a film's meaning in situ, which is only available through the experience of film-viewing itself. Furthermore, if a film's meanings are embedded within the film itself, what we choose to say about them will always be embedded in the historical moment in which we speak.

Another example I would like to offer here, from Vincente Minnelli's *Meet Me in St Louis* (1944), involves not so much a detail in the film's decor, such as the butterflies in *It's a Wonderful Life*, as a more cinematic device: the dissolve from Esther (Judy Garland), who has just finished singing a romantic song about the boy next door, to the pot of ketchup which her mother and the cook are making in the kitchen. Although it is possible to see the dissolve as a transitional device whose function is merely to move us from one scene to the next, it is nonetheless significant that at the point when Esther is most caught up in her romantic fantasies we should be reminded of the domestic drudgery involved in her mother's marriage, for there is no reason to suppose that Esther's marriage will be very different.

In pointing out the film's juxtaposition of the romantic with the ordinary, I am offering a juxtaposition of my own between the example of significant decor in *It's a Wonderful Life* and that of a significant cinematic device in *Meet Me in St Louis*, the point being that neither sort of meaning is completely pure. The suggestiveness of the butterflies depends in part on the camera's positioning of them in the same cinematic frame as Peter Bailey, while the dissolve in Minnelli's film only works because two distinct locations in the film's narrative world are being superimposed upon each other. Thus we shall discover through this book that although it is conceptually useful to distinguish between physical, dramaturgical and cinematic understandings of space, in practice they will be difficult to disentangle in our discussions of particular films, which involve a mutual reinforcement of meanings – or at least their interaction – in terms of all three conceptualisations of space simultaneously.

Equally difficult to disentangle will be our own spatial relationship, as spectators, to both the narrative world and the screen, which will form the focus of Chapter 4. Margaret Wertheim argues, in the context of her discussion of cyberspace, that 'When I go into cyberspace, my body remains at rest in my chair, but "I" – or at least some aspect of myself – am teleported into another arena which, while I am there, I am deeply aware has its own logic and geography' (1999: 228–9). Although her book makes passing reference to television, and she describes 'one of the functions of all great literature' as being 'to invoke believable "other" worlds' (49), oddly she has nothing to say about film, although much of what she does say is extremely suggestive. The extent to which we are able to be 'teleported' into the spaces of the filmic world or whether we can only view them from a separate space 'outside' will be a central concern of the final chapter of this book, as will the 'logic and geography' of that world, and our interactions with it.

Suggestions for further reading

Discussions of the meaning of 'meaning' are more prevalent within philosophy and linguistics than within film studies. However, Victor Perkins' work (1972; 1990) is helpful in setting out clearly the terms of the debate and its relevance to the analysis and understanding of films. For a contrasting view, see Bordwell (1989), with whom Perkins takes issue in his 1990 article. More recently, Gledhill and Williams (2000) include a number of articles from various writers who examine what is involved in attributing meaning to films.

1   SETTINGS: GEOGRAPHY, ARCHITECTURE, DECOR

In this chapter we will consider the usefulness of asking questions about the physical spaces within the narrative world, concentrating on spaces accessible to the characters themselves: the settings. At the most general level this will involve geographical location, although there is a sliding scale of generality even here: Europe or the United States, on the one hand, versus Boston or Tombstone, on the other, for example. After the broad geographical spaces have been mapped out, it will prove useful to look at how these places are further subdivided into significant locations within them: town and surrounding wilderness, saloon and church, night-club and courtroom, and so on. Even more specifically, the spaces within any given location will be laid out and individualised in terms of either natural features like mesas, rivers and trees, or architectural features like windows and doors, staircases and corridors – and their distinctiveness will be suggested and amplified by details in the decor. All of these things are worth noticing, although some films treat them more interestingly than others.

Of course it is neither possible nor desirable to match our observations too precisely to what the characters observe. We lack their freedom to walk around within these spaces and choose their own viewpoint. The fact that we are given access to the film's geography, architecture and decor from a predetermined set of positions inevitably shapes what we, as spectators, see, and influences what we make of it. However, this discussion will not only take account of aspects of the treatment of space which are inaccessible to the characters because we happen to be looking from a different spot, but also those which are necessarily inaccessible to them by their nature as fictional characters. For example we will find ourselves in a privileged position, as film spectators, to take account of effects which are the result of editing or camera position or the composition of the image, of which the characters, as characters, can never be aware. Such effects will be more properly treated in the chapter on specifically cinematic space which follows. However, our insights about the films would be artificially distorted were we to filter such things out, only talking about the film's world as if it were a 'real' physical space and not a cinematic one.

The investigative strategy will be one of selective emphasis rather than exclusion. We will start by asking: What sorts of geographical and architectural spaces seem to be significant in these films? How are these spaces structured and how do they relate to one another: are they seen as similar or as contrasting or as both? What sorts of characters are well-suited to inhabit them, and which are ill at ease? How do the spaces and their treatments relate to the thematic concerns of these films?

My Darling Clementine (John Ford, 1946)

The western is an obvious starting point in any consideration of the significance of geographical settings in American films, and the contrast between the western's wide open spaces and the social spaces of its settlements and homes has been extensively examined. Nevertheless, a given film may use such contrasting settings of wilderness and society and the boundary between them in very different ways and for extremely complex ends. My Darling Clementine, at first sight, may appear both traditional and schematic; the violence of the murderous Clantons presented as an aspect of that Western freedom from restraint which characterises the space beyond the frontier and which must be tamed by the civilising values associated both with the law – in the shape of Wyatt Earp (Henry Fonda) – and, more broadly, with the half-built church and the schoolhouse (still to be constructed) which are associated with the town's 'decent' citizens, a decency embodied above all in Clementine Carter (Cathy Downs), the woman from the East.

Overlaid upon the geographical structures of East and West and the values associated with each are narrative structures based on journeys and wanderings from place to place. In *My Darling Clementine*, various characters who have come to Tombstone from elsewhere explicitly question the sort of place Tombstone is and is likely to become (from Wyatt's recurring 'What kind of a town is this?' to the ironic tones of Doc Holliday (Victor Mature) when an English actor comes to town: 'Shakespeare in Tombstone'). Both Wyatt and Doc are participants in an ongoing debate about the sort of people who belong there or who need to be ejected. For example, Doc's suggestion to Clementine that Tombstone is no place for her 'kind of person' provides a tension with Wyatt's insistence that all decent people are welcome in the town, although it also provides a counter-current to Doc's own reaction to the prospect of Shakespeare in Tombstone, a prospect which he both recognises as incongruous and yet accepts gratefully and with dreamy wonderment when he later watches Thorndyke (Alan Mowbray) perform. Doc extends a courteous welcome to Thorndyke which he withholds from Clementine. Geographical and narrative concerns combine to facilitate an exploration of themes like progress and loss, as Eastern and Western values come into conflict, and the uneasy balancing act between them over time.

One difficulty in producing a neat schematic map of the film's spaces and structures in terms of a straightforward 'triumph' of Eastern law over Western violence, however, is that if the Clantons represent all that is worst in the West, Clementine is not a clear-cut representation of all that is best from the East. Her self-possession may suggest a coldness which is much less attractive than the full-blooded passion of her rival for Doc Holliday's love, the Western woman Chihuahua (Linda Darnell), the relative star-status of the two actresses favouring Chihuahua as well. Nevertheless, both women are vulnerable to humiliation at Doc's hands, so that their links through gender and their differences from the film's men provide another schema overlaid upon the film which tempers the structural contrasts between East and West. In any case, the East is more an idea than an onscreen space within the film, its values associated on the one hand with characters like Clementine, Doc and Thorndyke, and, on the other hand with specific settings – the church, the hotel, the barber's shop – within the growing western settlement of Tombstone in a period of transition from anarchy to law. The ambiguity involved in seeing East and West as, alternatively, geographical locations and sets of values, means that an Eastern character like Doc may be linked to a Western location like the saloon, while a Westerner like Wyatt may be associated with Eastern values like law and order. Both 'Western' and 'Eastern' locations abound within the western town, like the cattle range and the barber's shop respectively. To the extent that Doc renounces his Eastern past and Wyatt embraces a future intimately tied to Eastern values, the shift of Clementine's commitment from Doc to Wyatt is made possible, perhaps even inevitable.

Despite her lacking Chihuahua's outspokenness, Clementine appears to feel the effects of Doc's rejection at least as deeply as Chihuahua does, and Clementine's gentle reproof of Wyatt for his scant understanding of a woman's pride suggests that her apparent coldness may be more a self-protective strategy than evidence of a lack of passion. Indeed, pride may also motivate the ready transfer of her attentions to Wyatt, Clementine's request that he take her to the festivities at the church thus allowing her to display herself on his arm in front of all the decent folks in the town after her humiliating rejection by Doc. Ed Gallafent's claim that Doc's death at the O.K. Corral frees Clementine for Earp (1996: 305) is not quite accurate, for the transfer has already taken place well before then. Like Clementine, Chihuahua also takes comfort from another man, in her case Billy Clanton (John Ireland), after Doc has told her to leave him alone, although this is much less public than the transfer of Clementine's interest from Doc to Wyatt and thus implies a motivating physical desire on Chihuahua's part, rather than a need to save face.

A small detail from the film's decor may be taken to corroborate this sense that Clementine's lack of emotional expression may be calculated rather than naturally occurring: when she first catches up with Doc in the kitchen behind the bar, after trailing him from town to town, a pot is boiling on the stove behind her as they talk, its steam emphatically contrasting

FIGURE 2 *A pot boiling on the stove*

with the understated coolness of her manner yet, at the same time, encouraging us to be mindful of the emotional turmoil her measured delivery may be concealing, as she tells Doc she loves him and he insists she leave town: 'Very well, John,' she tells him without histrionics as they finish their conversation outside, 'I'll go'. So 'civilised' values of restraint and control are one thing for Wyatt and quite another for Clementine, who is so much more vulnerable as a woman on her own, and more needful of her pride and self-containment if her self-respect and 'decency' are to be preserved, thus making her a victim of such Eastern values as much as their champion. Where Wyatt, at least at the conscious level, seeks only to control others, the overwhelming object of Clementine's control is herself.

Taking notice of the contrasting geographical reference points in *My Darling Clementine* provides us with a useful starting point in sorting out its thematic terrain. However, detailed analysis may uncover other categories of sameness and difference (such as those of gender) derived from the film's narrative or its larger ideological context. These may be found to overlay the geographical reference points in ways which do not simply reinforce those implied by the generic setting alone but which may complicate and undercut them. Some examples of this have already been seen. To see how this works in more detail, close analysis of specific moments or sequences is essential; it will be useful to formulate more precisely the ways in which Doc and Wyatt are differently embedded in the spaces of the settings through the film's use of mirrors and reflections.

Chihuahua and Clementine have much in common – as women whose status depends at least in part on the patronage and protection of men – despite their initial associations with different geographical spaces (the West and East respectively). Clementine's tentative smile at Chihuahua when she first sees her in the saloon implies some awareness on her part of a potential alliance between them, despite Chihuahua's more guarded lack of response – her experience of making her way in the world not having prepared her to trust such disinterested gestures of friendship, and her precarious situation with Doc putting her on the alert for possible rivals. It may be useful to consider whether Doc and Wyatt are similarly linked through gender, although their respective relationships to East and West are harder to pin down. Doc Holliday is an Easterner who has lived for some time in the West and has abandoned many of the markers of his Eastern origins – such as his respectable profession as a doctor and the prestige that it entails – while Wyatt Earp was Marshal in Dodge City (another Western town somewhat further to the East) and is now a cattleman on his way to California (in the West), who resumes the role of lawman when his brother James (Don Garner) is killed. The film prepares the way both for Wyatt's alliance with Doc – by stressing shared aspects of their attitudes and positions within the film's patterns of symmetry and difference – and equally for Wyatt's ability to keep in some sort of balance the values of both East and West which, in Doc, produce irresolvable conflict.

One way in which the film links the two men is by making each of them the recipient of one of Chihuahua's songs, which she addresses to them in separate scenes in the saloon where she works, the words of the songs making pointed reference to their respective situations. The song she sings to Wyatt about 'cattle straying' after his herd has been rustled by the Clantons links gambling halls and cattle ranges in its lyrics shortly after Wyatt has agreed to be Marshal and has been asking questions about who controls gambling and cattle in the area (Doc and the Clantons respectively, thus linking Doc to the saloon within the town and the Clantons to the open range outside). Much more to the point, the line 'In gambling halls delaying, ten thousand cattle straying' may be a painful reminder to Wyatt who, after all, is playing poker while she sings. He too appears in no hurry to track down the rustlers who not only stole his cattle but killed his youngest brother James. This may explain his reaction as he listens and looks increasingly ill at ease, rather than any sense of suppressed desire for Chihuahua, as Gallafent argues (1996). In fact, the picture on the wall behind Wyatt of a boxer with fists raised in Chihuahua's direction suggests that, if anything, he is keeping his hostility towards her, rather than any amorous wishes, in check at that point, a hostility partly triggered by her song's reminder of his dereliction in his duty towards James. The ease with which he has fallen into a comfortable game of poker – taking his pleasures rather than doing his job – may remind us of Wyatt's earlier indulgence of his desire for a shave and a beer which led to James's death in the first place, when he was left behind to guard the cattle on his own. In contrast, Chihuahua's song for Doc, in a later scene, is explicitly about kisses, although its refrain that 'the first kiss is always the sweetest' is double-edged: since their relationship is long past 'the first kiss', what the song intends as an enticement – and which is performed as such – becomes just as strongly an admission of his waning interest in her and her probable impending loss. Indeed, it immediately provokes Doc's hurtful response, 'Why don't you go away? Squall your stupid little songs and leave me alone.'

Another link between the two men is the transfer of Clementine's interest from one man to the other (first Doc, then Wyatt), echoing and reversing Chihuahua's flirtatiousness towards each man in her musical numbers (first towards Wyatt, then Doc), again underlining that the women are symmetrically positioned as well as the men. This point is further emphasised in the scenes where Doc introduces Wyatt to each woman, in both cases discovering that Wyatt has met her before. Yet, despite such echoes and the symmetries between Wyatt and Doc with regard to the two women, as well as the ultimate alliance between them – where their potential antagonisms and rivalries are directed outward against the Clantons – an intractable difference between them remains which we can initially approach and try to understand in spatial terms.

In order to do this, it is useful to concentrate on two paired moments in the following sequence of scenes:

1   Clementine catches up with Doc and he tells her to leave town.

2   Doc stares at his framed diplomas in his darkened room and throws a glass at his own reflection.

3   Back in the bar, Chihuahua sings to Doc and he tells her to go away. She throws a glass at him and leaves, he continues to drink heavily and shoots at a lamp, and Wyatt knocks him out and drags him to his room.

4   Wyatt looks at himself in the barber's mirror, then at his reflection in the window outside. He is joined by his brothers (and, briefly, by some passing townsfolk on their way to church), his brothers leaving as Chihuahua walks by.

5   Chihuahua makes sure that Clementine is packing and then goes to Doc's room, where he decides to marry her.

6   Clementine asks Wyatt to take her to the celebrations at the half-built church.

A fade separates the first three scenes – which take place more or less continuously – from the next three, which also form a continuous block. The fade provides a transition from the evening before to the following morning. Retrospectively, we discover that the fade also functions to conceal within its darkness the beginning of Chihuahua's relationship with Billy Clanton, while she is on the rebound from Doc (who is unconscious in his room). These offscreen events provide the implicit spine of the sequence around which the explicit scenes before and after that night's events revolve. These six separate scenes can be paired in a variety of ways:

1 and 3   Doc rejects Clementine and Chihuahua respectively.
1 and 6   Doc rejects Clementine, Clementine pairs off with Wyatt.
2 and 4   Doc and Wyatt each stare at their own reflection.
3 and 5   Doc rejects Chihuahua, then decides to marry her.
5 and 6   Chihuahua and Clementine are paired off with Doc and Wyatt respectively.

In addition, there are more minor links (for example, Doc throws a glass at his reflection in 2, Chihuahua throws a glass at Doc in 3) and some of these scenes recall other scenes elsewhere in the film (for example, Chihuahua's singing to Doc in 3 echoes her singing to Wyatt much earlier). All of this may do little more than alert us to the fact that this is an intricately constructed narrative whose echoes and symmetries point us in the direction of important themes, many of which have already been discussed to some extent. It may be interesting to note how small a part the Clantons play in this section of the film and, indeed, more generally in much of what we have looked at so far. The film has far more on its mind than just their defeat; for example the divergent ways of experiencing and responding to the world which are available to women and men.

Looking more closely at the relationship between scenes 2 and 4 (the only two in the sequence not to be explicitly centred upon the heterosexual pairings and re-groupings of the four main characters in the sequence), we can explore more precisely what Doc and Wyatt see when they look at themselves, and what we observe when we watch them. The scene with Doc begins as he enters his darkened room. At the window to the left of Doc's diplomas on the wall, white lace curtains are bright with the sunlight of the everyday world outside, and sounds of music and of people enjoying themselves can be heard. The back-lit curtains playing slightly in the breeze are clean and indicative of a healthy world out of Doc's reach – beyond the window – as he sits on the bed in the shadows, staring at the diplomas which embody the distance between what he once was and what he has now become. As he stares at the juxtaposition of his reflected image within the frame with these remnants of his past – fresh from his rejection of Clementine's offer of the possibility of a reconstituted past back East –

he smashes the glass within the frame, providing visual confirmation of our growing sense of him as a shattered man beyond Clementine's power to heal. In the view of his reflection in the glass, nothing of the room around him can be seen – he appears as an isolated figure superimposed on the flat surface of the document inside the frame – and this 'erasure' of the actual space around him produces the impression that he is looking into an imagined past space which opens up to him behind the frame of the diploma whose glass he has smashed, rather than at a reflection of real physical space in the here and now.

His past is irretrievable, but the sunny present beyond the window – which appears to represent what Tombstone is able to offer him at its best – is equally presented as beyond Doc's grasp. The image of the white curtain at the window is inexplicably beautiful; perhaps as much so as the more famous sight, later in the film, of the half-finished church with the community around it which, as an image of hope and the future, is so much more heavily burdened with the weight of ideological consequence. Part of the poetry of the curtained window is its unobtrusiveness: the film is reticent about its significance and Doc himself never looks at it throughout the scene, so engrossed is he in his own much darker vision of his former self as lost and his present self as beyond redemption. Yet the continued silent presence of the folds of white lace moving in the breeze gives us some indication of the kind of clean and healthy dream from which he is excluded. His painful isolation and withdrawal into such a small space contrasts vividly with the celebration of communal harmony at the dedication of the church the following day. As Wyatt and Clementine walk to the church, space seems to open up around them, and we get our first sustained impression of the three-dimensionality of the town, an effect repeated in the way the other dancers move aside and open up a space for Wyatt and Clementine to dance in.

The barbershop scene where Wyatt examines himself in the mirror is very different from that of Doc in his room. The scene begins with a shot of horse-drawn wagons moving past the backdrop of Monument Valley with its dramatic mesas and buttes, then to Wyatt sitting in the barber's chair in front of a mirror that the barber is holding up in front of him, while more

FIGURE 3 *The harmony of town and nature*

people and wagons pass by the open door of the barbershop. Wyatt looks uncertain as he studies the fussy embellishments to his coiffure. As he walks past the shop-front outside, he turns to take another look at his reflection in the glass, adjusting his hat and straightening his tie with less uncertainty and a hint of satisfaction. In both instances his reflected image is surrounded by details of the offscreen space behind him, incorporating him firmly in the world around him rather than isolating him from it and abstracting him from space and time, as was the case with the reflected image of Doc Holliday in his darkened room. The reflection in the barber-shop window is especially striking in its simultaneous inclusion of an over-embellished Wyatt, the shop-front itself, and the reflections of both the townsfolk on their way to church and the landscape behind them: a perfect image of the reconciliation of East and West, town and landscape, artificial improvement and untouched natural beauty, with Wyatt at its centre as the focal-point and emblem of its harmonies.

Clementine's comment to Wyatt in the final scene of the sequence – 'I love your town in the morning, Marshal. It's so clean and clear' – could just as well apply to him, a point made even sharper when he responds to her admiration of the scent of the desert flower with the terse reply, 'That's my ... barber'. The clean, healthy world beyond the white curtain which is inaccessible to the tubercular Doc opens up to embrace Wyatt within its spaces and make him its own. Just before he stands up from the barber's chair, Wyatt stretches his legs out before him, as he will stretch out his arms to balance on the chair outside a few moments later. This is a world in which Wyatt can stretch and be comfortable. However, if Wyatt is the linchpin of a world of ease and reconciliation, it is also a world of surfaces and appearances, the reflection in the window flattening nature and society into a single plane. When Wyatt studies the details of his appearance (his pomaded hair, the set of his hat, his tie), it is not with too critical a gaze, but merely in order to make a few final adjustments while accepting his place within that world and looking no further than the present moment. There is no question of his contemplating anything deeper within himself or in his past, as Doc obviously does when he stares at himself and spits out a sarcastic 'Doctor John Holliday' at his image, before he smashes it to pieces. If Wyatt's reflection opens up a 'sideways' space – a sunny vision of harmonious surfaces spreading out around him and welcoming the spruced-up version of Wyatt at its centre – then the image of Doc that is presented is both narrower and deeper, drawing him into its temporal and psychological depths while simultaneously insisting on his present spatial constriction as he hunches over on the bed in the shadows of his darkened room. He occupies a much smaller space than Wyatt in the real spaces of the physical world, yet has an understanding of darker realities beneath its appearances which are inaccessible to Wyatt and wilfully suppressed by Clementine.

So, although Wyatt is a positive figure in a world seen as full of promise, the film is quite clear about his limitations in taking people at face value. These produce the most unpleasant moments in the film: when he throws Indian Charlie out of town ('Indian, get out of town and stay out'), and when he threatens to run Chihuahua back to the Apache reservation where he tells her she belongs (although she is Mexican rather than Apache, a fine distinction of no importance to Wyatt in terms of his superficial sense of 'us' and 'them').

Wyatt's inability or refusal to look more deeply puts him at a serious disadvantage in his first meeting with Pa Clanton (Walter Brennan) and his son Ike (Grant Withers), when Wyatt's trust in Pa Clanton's surface friendliness prevents him from realising that he himself is paving the way for his brother's death by letting Clanton know that Wyatt and his brothers (all but James, as it turns out) might go into town for a shave and a beer that night. His frankness strikes us as particularly ill-advised in light of the sinister music that introduces the Clantons, the change in Pa Clanton's manner when Wyatt turns up, and Ike's openly intimidating stare. Further, in all the shots of Pa Clanton on his own, Ike's hand remains visible in the bottom right-hand corner of the shot, his fingers curled menacingly around the loops of his rope, even though the rest of him is excluded from the frame and his father is at his most friendly in his conversation with Wyatt. So we are let in on the limitations in Wyatt's ways of seeing the world, rather than merely sharing them. This split between our point of view and Wyatt's is also evident in his response to Clementine, whom he recognises as a 'lady' (with all that entails) from the moment she steps off the stage, taking her performance of this role – while accurate enough in terms of her social positioning – as evidence of her nature through and through. Such an assumption is undermined by the access which the film gives us to a depth and complexity of feeling within her, which her public enactment of a lady-like self-possession and lack of passion allows her to keep under wraps.

The potential violence of the Clantons and its eruption at various points in the film, to which Wyatt is initially so blind and which he remains reluctant to acknowledge, delays that reconciliation of East and West within the film's narrative world which Wyatt already seems to embody within himself. We are given numerous examples of his responding to conflict and the threat of violence with easy reasonableness and friendly persuasion, rather than with anger or gunplay. Thus, when Doc insists he have a glass of champagne, despite his stated preference for whiskey, he agrees ('Champagne it is'); when the men at the theatre want to ride the theatre's manager around town on a rail when Thorndyke fails to turn up, he persuades them to let him find Thorndyke and bring him back instead; when Doc offers him a drink after discovering that Clementine has tracked him down, and refuses to take no for an answer, as if spoiling for a fight, Wyatt affably defuses the tension ('No, thanks, I just finished supper'); and when Doc interrupts Clementine's dinner to ask why she has not yet left town, Wyatt invites him to join them for the meal.

His reluctance to confront the Clantons, where violence must be met with violence and cannot be so effortlessly defused, is consistent with his choice of ease and adaptation over strife and confrontation in almost every other context: stretching his legs in the barber's chair, submitting to the barber's improvements with no loss of dignity, relaxing into a game of poker or a drink rather than embracing an ethic of hard work, and generally complaining when bullets, cheats, or songs intrude upon his desire for a shave or a quiet game of poker. Not only is he playing cards when he might better seek the killer of his brother James, but he has just finished enjoying a drink when Pa Clanton dumps the body of his brother Virgil (Tim Holt) back in town. Having sent Virgil off to find Billy Clanton after Billy shoots Chihuahua, Wyatt not only does not ride after him to back him up, but appears to have put his brother's danger completely out of his mind as he lingers in the saloon. His approach to being Marshal seems to fit the description of his job, given by a man on his way to the celebrations at the church as 'keeping the peace' rather than enforcing the law.

Winston Miller, the film's scriptwriter, acknowledges the unconventional aspect of the script's depiction of Wyatt Earp:

It violated all the rules. Earp comes to Tombstone, decides not to be sheriff, his brother is killed, and he stays to find the killer. It's the only reason he stays. For five reels he doesn't do a damn thing about it. He sits on the porch with his feet up, and you have John Ford vignettes. You have interesting scenes, but there's no urgency, just a lot of shambling around. (Quoted in Ronald L. Davis (1995: 191))

Wyatt's ease and lack of urgency, which this quotation confirms, provide a contrast with Doc's lack of ease, a 'dis-ease' which is given a vivid physical form through his literal disease, his coughs often disrupting moments of apparent reconciliation and resolution: for example after Doc pulls a gun on Wyatt, who responds by introducing his brothers, and Doc invites them to join him for a friendly drink, or when Doc takes over Thorndyke's performance of Hamlet's soliloquy and even the Clanton brothers stand by in silence. But as long as the Clantons remain alive, Wyatt's success as a harmonising force will never be complete, and the chance of a healthy community will be spoilt by the Clantons' presence in its midst.

When Doc and Wyatt arrive at Chihuahua's room and interrupt her and Billy Clanton, it is noteworthy that the door through which she hurries Billy out is covered by a white lace curtain, like the one in Doc's room earlier, and Billy shoots her from offscreen – from the space behind the door – when she implicates him in the murder of James, thus clearing Doc. So the shining vision of Tombstone's future in the earlier scene is now shown to harbour killers within it in Tombstone's present, and they cannot be silenced by friendly persuasion alone.

The scene in which Thorndyke performs Hamlet's soliloquy is also relevant. If the prospect of Shakespeare in Tombstone fills Doc with grateful wonder, it is an impromptu performance away from the main event – the scheduled performance of 'The Convict's Oath' at the theatre from which Thorndyke is playing absentee – indicating that Thorndyke, like Doc, has seen better days and, like Doc in his resumption of the doctor's role when he operates unsuccessfully on Chihuahua, Thorndyke turns in a 'botched' performance of a role played long ago and only half-remembered. Both men's pasts in the East provide the substance of Tombstone's future in the West, but a future held in abeyance as long as the lawless Clantons are around. Indeed, apart from the bemused Mexicans in the saloon, and Doc and Wyatt, the Clanton brothers are the only other witnesses to Thorndyke's recitation and the instigators of its disruption: 'Shakespeare was not made for taverns,' Thorndyke tells us as he leaves the room with Wyatt, 'nor for tavern louts.'

FIGURE 4 *Ike Clanton walking to his death*

Even Wyatt stands by and listens out of respect and good manners rather than understanding, Doc alone feeling the resonance of Thorndyke's performance. When Doc picks up the lines where Thorndyke stumbles, Hamlet's reference to death as 'The undiscovered country from whose bourn no traveller returns' is especially meaningful in the context of the western, a genre of journeys and geography. However, Doc's journey towards death is very different from Wyatt's earlier journey to the town, although the name of Tombstone applies equally well to both destinations. Appropriately, Doc and the Clantons die together at the O.K. Corral, while the remaining Earp brothers, Wyatt and Morgan (Ward Bond), both survive. Ike Clanton's walk into a wall of smoke – gun raised as he meets his death – is a darkly poetic illustration of Hamlet's words, and the visual effects recall the smoke that swirls around Doc both as he delivers those words and elsewhere in the film. Although Ike is the meanest-looking villain in the piece, his death and

Doc's are two of a kind, each in his own way excluded from Tombstone's future and contrasted with Wyatt's gentleness and geniality which, through Henry Fonda's performance – his voice, his walk, his face – imbue the film with another kind of poetry, a poetry of harmonious surfaces and ease in the world.

From a consideration of space in *My Darling Clementine*, we arrive at some thoughts about time and mortality, along the way observing how gender differences were overlaid upon the film's spatial mappings of East and West, town and wilderness. In the final scene of the film, Wyatt says goodbye to Clementine and says he will be back, but he shows little understanding of the way that their experiences of space and time may differ. As he sets off on his travels, we know that his purposeful journey will make the time pass quickly, while her remaining in one place as she waits for his return will make the intervening time stand still.

Party Girl (Nicholas Ray, 1958)

If the geographical setting of the frontier is central to the western, with its interest in an American continent in the process of losing its open spaces to the ambiguous advance of civilised forces from the East, then the modern city is at the heart of the gangster film. As with representations of the American West, so too have representations of the American city received extensive critical attention, especially with respect to film noir, the collective name for those bleak explorations of male anxiety which dominated the genre in the 1940s and 1950s. Although *Party Girl* falls within that period (appearing the same year as Orson Welles' *Touch of Evil*, which is often cited as the last notable example of film noir), the fact that it is a widescreen gangster film in colour immediately distinguishes it from the noir strand of the genre which was just coming to an end. The film has links with other colour melodramas of the period – often widescreen as well – as much as with the gangster film per se, with the 1950s producing some of the finest examples of small-town family melodramas by directors such as Douglas Sirk (*All That Heaven Allows*, 1956), Vincente Minnelli (*Some Came Running*, 1959), and, of course, Ray himself (*Rebel Without a Cause*, 1955).

One effect of these cross-generic links is to position *Party Girl* away from the obsessive male-centredness of gangster films in the noir tradition. Salient within it are the interests of the classy night-club dancer, Vicky Gaye (Cyd Charisse), and not just those of the corrupt mob lawyer, Tommy Farrell (Robert Taylor), with whom she falls in love. Their shared journey from cynicism and corruption to a surprisingly upbeat mutual redemption at the end acts both to structure the narrative and to balance its point of view between male and female perspectives and concerns. The film's title, along with that of *My Darling Clementine*, emphasises the importance of the central female character in these examples from what are traditionally male-centred genres, although Vicky's profession and initial presentation imply she is a 'saloon girl' like Chihuahua, rather than a 'lady' like Clementine.

Similarly, Tommy seems more like the troubled and introspective Doc Holliday, rather than like Wyatt Earp. Both Doc and Tommy have tarnished the promise of their pasts and both men's bodies bear the marks of their moral imperfections, in the form of illness or injury. *Party Girl* is explicit in linking Tommy's criminal entanglements with his tangled limbs – he describes himself to Vicky as 'a crippled attorney with a crippled reputation' – and his decisions to get his legs straightened and to 'go straight' are seen as parts of a single process. Yet whereas Chihuahua and Doc are dead at the end of *My Darling Clementine*, both killed by the Clantons' bullets, Vicky and Tommy have been 'cleansed' and transformed into a couple with a future – more like Clementine and Wyatt, in this respect – by the end of *Party Girl*. However, while Wyatt remains a man of superficial vision, and Clementine continues to hide her feelings beneath a veil of judiciously chosen words, a set of differences which culminate in their unacknowledged asymmetrical relationships to space and time in the final shot, Vicky and Tommy achieve something much closer to mutual understanding and acceptance. Both are given an intelligence and maturity which are exceedingly rare, especially for men, in American film depictions of heterosexual romance.

The city in question is Chicago in the 1930s, although its appearance is glossy rather than gritty, its settings largely interiors rather than urban streets. The main structural pairings and oppositions are between one particular location within the city and another (for example, night-club versus courtroom, train compartment versus jail, and so on), rather than between the city as a whole and another contrasting space. The two exceptions to this are California, which is presented as an offscreen place of potential safety for Vicky and the chance of a fresh start, and Europe, where Tommy goes to be cured. Although the use of a place out West to represent hope and new beginnings is unsurprising (it forms the basis for many westerns, after all), what is more unusual is the use of Europe to represent not only healing but a vision of nature and civilisation in harmony (a vision which is also common to the western, as we saw in *My Darling Clementine*, but is generally seen as a peculiarly American synthesis, and not at all what Europe usually stands for in American films). The trees, mountains, green fields, and sea in the background of the shots where Tommy and Vicky are reunited abroad after his cure concentrate on the picturesque qualities of nature wholly lacking in the rest of the film.

Given that the settlement of the American continent is usually represented as an East-to-West affair, with Europe as the ultimate eastern site of embarkation, Europe has tended to be seen as a place of traditional high culture, social hierarchies, and the accumulated customs and practices of the past, from which the westward journey provides a liberating and essentially democratic break. However, this view of Europe as the old country and America as the new is not merely a back-to-nature model of the journey west, but a model of a future involving transcendence of nature as America becomes increasingly identified with such qualities as material progress and driving ambition, outstripping Europe with its youthful vigour and achievement. So if America sees itself as younger and newer than Europe, any sense of this as implying a more primitive condition is overturned by the mythologising of twentieth-century America as more modern, forward-thinking and dynamic in its more positive manifestations, and more oppressive and corrupt in its more negative forms, a matter of modern, technologised forms of violence (both in the shape of gang warfare and the enforcement of the law) rather than the primitivism of nature in the raw. The American city, correspondingly, has been inflected in both positive and negative versions but, in its negative form, it makes possible a reconceptualisation of Europe in terms of a more leisurely, old-fashioned way of life which escapes the corruptions of the modern cities to the west. To see Europe nostalgically in this way is to hold an openly critical view of at least some aspects of what America has become and implies a wish to unmake time and return to an earlier period, displacing a nostalgia for America's past onto a mythified utopian version of Europe's present.

Vincente Minnelli's *Brigadoon* (1954) is a musical which idealises Europe in the form of a magical village in the Scottish highlands which only comes alive one day every hundred years, and is thus insulated from the corruptions of time. This is contrasted with a materialistic version of modern New York from which its main character, Tommy Albright (Gene Kelly) seeks to escape. When he returns to Brigadoon for good, his plane flying from New York to Scotland, we see it moving from right to left across the screen. Although this seems odd in terms of geography alone – since the usual convention in map-making is to locate the East on the right and the West on the left – it makes perfect sense as a visualisation of a journey into the past, where the conventional representation of time's movement from the present to the past is from right to left. Although *Party Girl* does not present Europe in quite so literal a way as a piece of the past, the time that Vicky and Tommy spend there together is just as much an escape from twentieth-century America and all it represents at its worst.

The 'picturesque' qualities in Ray's depiction of Europe's beauty spots were discussed earlier, the term implying the unconvincing, constructed aspects of their presentation, their 'too-good-to-be-true' qualities. The contrast between surface appearances and what lies beneath or behind them is a central theme throughout the film, linking Vicky's performances at 'The Golden Rooster', for example, with Tommy's performances in court. However, in both cases we are given access to the work and calculation behind the polished public performances, the 'scaffolding' on which they hang. Thus, the first number at the night-club – with its glamorous women and gaudy gold-coloured costumes – is followed by backstage shots of a bare wooden staircase and plain brick walls, with the showgirls tightly packed into the cramped space between the rows of make-up mirrors in the dressing room.

FIGURE 5 *Rico in his study: curtains, chair, books*

Similarly, Tommy's first appearance in court is preceded by our view of him swapping watches so that he can win the jury's sympathy with a casual reference to the pocket watch he says his father gave him, and he openly admits to Vicky afterward that he exaggerated his limp to similar purpose. The emphasis on Tommy's legs is matched by an emphasis on the show-girls' legs in their opening performance, a performance which is little more than a display of their bodies as they parade around the stage, just as Tommy displays his body in court. When Rico (Lee J. Cobb) threatens to break Tommy's bones beyond repair and to destroy Vicky's beautiful face with acid he shows that, in his eyes at least, these aspects of their market-ability as performers are what they must surely value most.

Rico Angelo is another sort of performer and his apartment is another sort of stage. Its decor is lush and theatrical, and this is particularly notice-able in several scenes in his study, where he sits at his desk in a tasselled chair covered in red brocade – a chair that looks more like a throne – with layers of thick gathered curtains at the window behind him and cases full of books along an adjoining wall, which we must presume are for appear-ance's sake, since he is no intellectual. The apartment, although roomy, is over-decorated with patterned wallpaper, mirrors and ornaments, and crowded with people when we dissolve from the dressing room at the night-club in the opening scene to the party at Rico's which follows, generating an atmosphere of claustrophobia and vulgar ostentation. Among the guests are numerous showgirls – including Vicky – who have been paid to turn up, so even the party guests are fake.

Vicky is singled out not just by her brightly coloured dress and by the fact that she had been described as 'expensive merchandise' at the club when Rico's henchmen were shopping for guests, but by her refusal to stay at the party when Louis Canetto (John Ireland), who paid her to turn up, starts making a play for her. Tommy, in turn, is contrasted with the other men by his aloofness from the party and its glamorous female 'guests', as he talks with a small group of respectable well-dressed men, turning round so we can see him only when a gunshot rings out, as Rico shoots a framed photograph of Jean Harlow and Tommy responds with open sarcasm: 'Nice shooting, Rico, where'd you get her? Between the eyes?' Tommy decides to leave soon after, and agrees to drop Vicky off, both of them linked by their critical attitude to men who treat women as no more than beautiful objects to be appropriated or destroyed.

Each has reason to be wary when they first meet. Vicky has already articulated her self-protective attitude to men – 'Never get crowded into a corner ... never let them get too close' – in the earlier dressing-room scene when she explained to her roommate Joy how this had happened before – 'Just once, in a dark and dirty little barn back home in Oklahoma ... I was fifteen'. Tommy too has learned a lesson in the past, when he married a showgirl who was attracted to his money but disgusted by his crooked legs, and who now refuses to divorce him. So the relationship between Vicky and Tommy develops in a context of mutual resistance and watchfulness, as they gradually notice aspects of each other and reveal aspects of themselves behind the performances on stage and in court which are all that the rest of the world can see.

In a way their relationship develops backwards, unlike those melodramas where the couple fall in love and then discover secrets about each other which threaten to push them apart. Here, what Vicky and Tommy each come to know is the underlying goodness and trustworthiness of the other which, once established, is never under threat from within the relation-ship, the only threat to their future coming from outside, from mobster and lawman alike, each of whom exploits the potential deceptiveness of the visible world for revenge or personal gain. For example, Rico pretends to host a dinner in honour of a crook who has betrayed him, in order to try to beat him to death with the award (a miniature silver pool cue), and the State's Attorney Jeffrey Steward (Kent Smith) releases Tommy from jail so that Rico will assume he has talked, in order to get Tommy to do precisely that as the price of keeping Vicky safe. The manipulation of appearances is everywhere around them.

It is helpful to examine the development of the relationship between Vicky and Tommy in more detail, using close analysis of particular moments to explore the way that narrative and setting combine to reinforce some of the themes we have explored. Although some of these themes have their counterparts in *My Darling Clementine* their treatment and significance are noticeably different. Where the presentation of the visible world in Ford's film is a harmonious one which reconciles its conflicting elements (at least once the Clantons are dead) so that the narrative world by the end of the film is a fitting one for Wyatt Earp to inhabit, it is not so clear that Vicky and Tommy will find a place to nurture their romance, even when Rico, Louis and the others are dead. The world of *Party Girl* is much more overtly repressive, misogynistic, and self-serving, and those on the right side of the law are just as complicit as those on the wrong.

Since Vicky and Tommy's relationship develops throughout the film and, even in the early stages, encompasses many scenes, it is practical to exam-ine a few key moments rather than all the relevant scenes in their entirety. They first meet at Rico's apartment, when Vicky asks Tommy for his help in getting away from the party, which Louis had paid her to attend. Although he initially refuses, he agrees when he decides to leave, after Rico's shoot-ing of Jean Harlow's photograph. As he drops her by her apartment, she invites him inside. This is the first moment which warrants closer examina-tion, since the details of Cyd Charisse's delivery of the lines are crucial to our understanding of what is going on.

FIGURE 6 *I could make you some ... uh ... cocoa*

The offer of a drink associated with childhood and cosy domesticity is made with self-conscious irony: 'Would you like to come in for a minute? There's not much in the icebox, but I could make you some ... uh ... cocoa'. Charisse pauses before the final word and gestures with a wave of her hand, as if looking for the right way to communicate what she means, which is something like a combination of 'Now let's see, how shall I put this?' with a more collusive 'Let's call it cocoa', and yet simultaneously conveys a wish to confound his expectations – by actually giving him cocoa – at the moment of apparently confirming them, which again can be translated as something like 'Yes, I'll invite you up, but don't assume you know what to expect'. He is momentarily taken aback by her offer, but then smiles appreciatively and plays along: 'Cocoa? I haven't had any cocoa since I was nine years old. Maybe you've got a new recipe'. There is real warmth and a hint of self-deprecation in Tommy's inflections and smile, a sort of verbal and visual shrug, as though he would like to relate to Vicky in a less brittle and ironic fashion, but will follow her lead, thus smoothing the way towards what looks set to be a superficial relationship of wittily coded conversations and ironicised domesticity – like so much else in the film, a matter of performance, although here by mutual consent – in line with Vicky's earlier

FIGURE 7 *Vicky collectively sedated*

comments to Joy about keeping men at a distance. Throughout the conversation the vertical strut of the car separates them, framing each in a separate space as they trade clever remarks.

However, the emotionally uninvolving flirtation is disrupted by Vicky's
discovery of Joy's suicide, finding her dead in the bath upstairs. The heavy
velvet curtains at Rico's party are replaced by the simple shower curtain in
the right of the shot, and Rico's symbolic destruction of Jean Harlow, when
he shoots her photograph because she 'betrayed' him by her marriage,
is replaced by the brutally real self-destruction of the pregnant showgirl
whose married lover has abandoned her. Although Rico shoots the woman
he sees as having abandoned him, whereas Joy kills herself because of
her lover's betrayal, women remain the victims of men in both cases. This
implication of women being at the mercy of male power and control is more
mildly recapitulated when Vicky is collectively sedated at the hospital by a
doctor, a policeman, and Tommy himself, although Tommy's taking charge
of her is motivated by convincing, if somewhat business-like, concern.

When he takes her back to his apartment and she falls asleep on the
couch, he covers her with her coat; another gesture – like her offer of cocoa
– which both evokes childhood and yet is not completely innocent, Tommy
taking advantage of her unconsciousness to give her a good looking over
first. Not only are these present evocations of childhood simultaneously

vehicles for Vicky's and Tommy's respective desires, but what we learn of their actual childhoods reveal scenarios of violent injury and lasting trauma (the sexual assault endured by Vicky in the corner of an Oklahoma barn, and Tommy's fall from the bridge which crushed his hip). These are no idealised pasts remembered with affection. The most hopeful aspect of the paired regressions is not just the genuineness of Tommy's protective gesture in tucking her in, but the fact that the mention of cocoa reminds Tommy of being nine years old, a time before his accident at the age of twelve, so the healing process that will take place in Europe, whose regressive character has been noted earlier, is already implicit in the early stages of the relationship, with Vicky as its source.

Whereas Rico's infatuation with Jean Harlow is shallow and inconsequential, the emotional cost of Joy's affair is profound, and the sense of life-and-death issues replacing superficial emotional involvement and behaviour relates to Vicky as well, as her defensive breeziness gives way, in the aftermath of Joy's death, producing the first breakthrough in Vicky's and Tommy's relationship, though more for her than for him. Despite Tommy's thoughtful concern for Vicky, he continues to make easy assumptions about her showgirl past, and although his assumptions about the sort of modelling she's done – 'calendar art, girlie magazines' – are accurate enough, as Vicky readily admits, another side to her has begun to show through. This is most immediately apparent when she asks him to take the money she got from Louis Canetto and return it to him on her behalf. When he asks her why, and she explains that she wants him to have a better opinion of her, he calls it a sentimental gesture and refuses. She then sits in on his courtroom defence of Louis on a murder charge and asks him afterwards 'What makes you so much better than me?' Although he is unapologetic about his sentimental rhetoric in court, her angry offer of pity – with its implication that he is pitiful – provokes his anger in return: 'Get outta here,' he growls, but it is a turning point in the process of his redemption, just as her roommate's suicide was for her. Again there is a pleasing balance in the treatment of the two of them; each is transformed through a refusal to embrace the role of victim, each galvanised by a need for the other's respect. Seeing Vicky give Louis back the money on her way out of the speakeasy where she had followed Tommy after the trial, he echoes her action by giving Louis the pocket watch he had used in court.

Just as Vicky had observed Tommy in the courtroom, now Tommy observes her performance at the club. Although he had got her the solo work so that she would not have to parade half-naked in the chorus, the number is no great improvement, as she peels off her skirt and scarf in a partial striptease, defiantly addressing her look and actions to him. The unapologetic way that each of them makes clear to the other exactly what it is that they do makes it possible for them to begin to look beyond each other's performative selves and to expose and explore the more vulnerable selves underneath. In a similar vein, he tells her he is married because 'I wanted to tell you. I wanted you to know'. It is a measure of their accept-ance of each other – flaws and all – that she continues to work at the club and he continues to work for Rico long after their relationship has begun. In an ironic twist at the film's dénouement, Tommy uses all of his rhetorical powers – until then used merely to defend the guilty – to save Vicky and himself, by persuading Rico that he needs Tommy's help. Tommy promises to rip his own testimony against Rico to shreds from behind the scenes, advising Rico's new lawyer every step of the way.

Vicky's and Tommy's growing acknowledgement that there is no essen-tial corruption beneath the other's flawed public self culminates in the affecting moment when Vicky leaves the club and sees Tommy waiting by his car. There is an almost balletic quality to the way Charisse uses her body here, as she pauses and then moves towards him – unsmiling, but with a dancer's grace. The wind is blowing her hair and rippling the fur collar of her coat, as other passers-by hold on to their hats – inspired details which make it appear as if Vicky is being helped towards Tommy by the breeze – and neither says a word as he holds open the door of his car and she gets in. The harmony of his actions and hers – the sense of unquestioning mutual acceptance – and the apparent collusion of nature itself give their coming together a dreamlike quality, transcending their earlier defensive-ness and self-justifications. Another moving aspect of the scene is the way that Tommy offers himself as a passively waiting figure, rather than an actively appropriating one. The assumption of men's right to appropriate women elsewhere in the film has been inextricably linked to a masculine desire to control and exploit.

The car stops by a bridge which is on the point of opening, the bridge's massive mechanism dwarfing them as it rises behind them. Tommy explains that, as a twelve-year-old kid, he and the other boys would hang on the girders as the bridge opened, to see who had the most nerve, until one day he slipped and got mixed up in the gears. From a shot of the bridge closing again, the scene dissolves to Tommy's apartment as he continues his story looking out of the window in the foreground of the shot, with Vicky seated on the couch in the room behind him, and Tommy explains how his need to succeed quickly was part of his wish to be whole again.

This is a key scene for several reasons. It is another example of the film revealing what was earlier described as the 'scaffolding' on which its surface world depends – the stark and powerful structure of the bridge, in whose gears Tommy got caught up, is an apt reminder of the underlying social structures which control their lives. That Tommy's accident was the result of male competitiveness and bravado gone wrong (like Buzz's death in the 'chickee run' in *Rebel Without a Cause*) suggests that those structures are fundamentally to do with the performance of gender, which has its equivalents for Vicky too. Later, at the doctor's office, when Vicky and Tommy seek a cure for his injuries, the X-ray of his bones exposes the skeletal structures of his body – a sort of internal scaffolding – and Vicky finds out from the doctor's remarks that Tommy has been living in extreme physical pain. So, in parallel with the couple opening up to one another, the film reveals the mechanisms of the social world it depicts, peeling back its glossy surface to expose its ideological structures and at the same time revealing the pain behind individual presentations of self in that world.

In light of Tommy's account of his childhood accident, his comment about the pocket watch in court – 'My father gave me this watch when I was a kid … in City Hospital' – is no longer quite so straightforward an example of rhetorical persuasion. The reference to being a kid in hospital now seems to imply that there is some truth to the story after all, a conclusion reinforced later, when he tells Rico a story about a weak kid given a watch by his father, which Rico restored when a big guy took it away: 'I was the kid'. At that point Tommy displays his watch to illustrate his words, and we realise that the watch from his father may be the one he removes before his court appearances, not the dime-a-dozen pocket watches he actually presents as such in court. Similarly, Vicky's earlier offer of cocoa may disguise, through her ironic manner, a more genuine desire to settle down. In fact, when we see her backstage with Joy near the start of the film, she is repairing her dress with a needle and thread, and we later see her at Tommy's, after he has left for Europe, with the refrigerator prominent in the frame behind her, implying that she fits within a domestic space more comfortably than we may have assumed.

Another noteworthy aspect of the scene by the bridge is its treatment of time, since the dissolve from the bridge to Tommy's apartment, by preserving the continuity of his words, implies a magical unity of time across space in line with the dreamy representation of their romance elsewhere. The scene ends with Tommy offering to take her home, Vicky approaching him and letting her coat fall to the floor, and Tommy picking it up. The moment is poised on the ambiguities of his response to her clear offer to stay, his look of reciprocating desire belied by his actions as he drapes the coat on her shoulders and follows her out. When we dissolve to a backstage scene at the club, in which she opens a box of roses, his note – 'For the happiest months of my life' – clears up any doubts. Time is no longer a burden to be endured and got through as quickly as possible, as Tommy's previous attitude has implied (telling the jury he will not waste their time, informing Vicky he is 'a great believer in the quickest way', and so on). Rather, it has now become a bountiful gift, although its pleasures are experienced offscreen. The year of his medical treatment in Europe, although physically painful, is part of the same healing process, and it also unfolds offscreen, although culminating in the onscreen montage which marks their reunion.

So their relationship is represented in a number of ways. The most memorable moments in the development of their romance often show them either moving as if in a dream or poised in a kind of watchful stillness. Alternatively, the romance is given the unconvincing picturesque quality of the European idyll, or is pushed offscreen. The cumulative effect of these decisions is to present the romance as a thing apart, with no place to shelter it in the 'real' spaces of the narrative world. Indeed, after the return from Europe, the world back home is as manipulative as ever, its mechanisms still firmly in place. Although Vicky and Tommy are less frequently seen against elaborate theatrical backgrounds and decor, they are more often located within bare geometrical settings (such as the jail and the train compartment), and are frequently enclosed by grids or bars, and placed in settings dominated by parallel lines. Even before their return, we know the European trip is at an end, when Tommy takes a phone call from Rico in a booth which encloses him like a cage, although the oppressive nature of this world is more starkly and insistently exposed once they return.

The question as to whether their relationship can survive in such a world remains. In *My Darling Clementine*, the killing of the Clantons gives the town of Tombstone a new and brighter future. In *Party Girl*, however, where the law itself is corrupt and the ideological mechanisms of the film's narrative world produce masculinities which feed on competition and inflict terrible pain, the killing of gangsters is simply not enough. The montage of gangland murders which 'answers' the idyllic montage of Tommy and Vicky in Europe after his cure, and the extraordinary excess of Rico's death (spilling acid on himself and falling from the window, as the police spray the building with bullets) are evidence of both the extent and the enormous power of the obstacles in the way. Added to this must be the self-satisfaction of the smiling State's Attorney, with his eye on a Senate seat, in the final moments of the film.

Suggestions for further reading

Key texts for understanding the cultural significance of the American landscape – especially the frontier and the wilderness beyond it – are Leo Marx (1964) and Henry Nash Smith (1950), while Morton and Lucia White (1977) provide a good account of changing attitudes to the city. In addition, many studies of the western (for example Buscombe and Pearson (1998); Cameron and Pye (1996)) and of film noir (Hirsch (1981); Thomas (1992a)) give some attention to the specific generic uses made of the nineteenth-century western landscape and the modern American city respectively.

2   DRAMATURGICAL SPACES: ONSTAGE AND OFFSTAGE, PUBLIC AND PRIVATE

The emphasis in the previous chapter was on the physical spaces within the narrative world, focusing on examples from two genres where settings are all-important: the western and the gangster film. This is not to say that settings are insignificant in other genres, but merely that they may be less explicitly tied to our sense of the genre per se, although equally available as bearers of significance in individual films. Thus horror films or musicals, say, may take place without generic strain in either East or West, and may be set in either city, town, or country. Yet films of any genre, including these, may use the details of their settings in meaningful and expressive ways.

This chapter concentrates on examples of small-town family melodrama, a less tightly constituted genre than the western or the gangster film, and one which has been labelled somewhat arbitrarily, partly to indicate that the setting is, once again, a crucial aspect, although other terms (such as 'domestic melodrama') have often been used to call attention to more or less the same films. The small-town settings of such melodramas may be seen as descendants of the western's settlements – versions of what places like Tombstone go on to become – once they have been well and truly brought within the rule of law. However, although this is an important aspect of these films, a further set of issues will be explored. The small town is an implicit stage along the way from Tombstone to Chicago; a place where the lawlessness of the old West has been suppressed and the technological violence of the modern city has not yet developed.

This way of construing the small town – as a place where dreams of both the old West and the modern city are uneasily suppressed, yet continually threaten to re-emerge – can be seen most dramatically in Capra's *It's a Wonderful Life*. On the one hand, George Bailey is linked to western imagery, both in his desire to 'lasso the moon' and, less positively, in his diminishment to a cartoon cowboy in his girlfriend Mary's drawing of him doing exactly that. However, George is also shown that, had he never been born, the small town of Bedford Falls would have become, precisely, the film-noir city of Pottersville which, rather than being contrasted with Bedford Falls as a different space, is merely its other aspect (that is, Pottersville is the potential within Bedford Falls which was always there and will continue to inhabit it). A theme of doubleness is similarly built into many other interesting depictions of small-town family life.

We will work back to such issues from an initial concentration on dramaturgical spaces, rather than focussing on such concrete physical spaces as the city or town or any particular locations within them. That is, the opposition between characters who are 'onstage' and those who are 'offstage' will be taken to refer not just to whether they are in a literal theatre and on a literal stage but, more metaphorically, to whether they are putting on a face and taking on a role for the benefit of others, or are revealing something like an 'authentic' self that lies beneath the surface presentation. Such issues are by no means specific to small-town family melodramas alone.

The staginess of many American films – the theatricality of their treatments of setting and decor, the explicitness with which their characters are shown to enact social roles, and the importance of gesture and pose – suggests that such an opposition between onstage and offstage moments might be central to their construction of a viewer point of view, regardless of specific genre. In fact, the technique of allowing the viewer behind the scenes in order to give us privileged access to a character's 'true' feelings or motives (for example by letting us remain with a character after everyone else has left a room or by bringing to our notice an explanatory detail in the decor) is a fairly obvious and widespread strategy fundamental to any film's ability to qualify and comment upon the characters it presents. Nevertheless, two aspects of this strategy appear to be more salient in small-town family melodramas than in other sorts of film: firstly the overwhelming sense that their characters are constituted by their roles and that there is no further 'authentic' self to be found, and secondly that they are motivated, above all, by a desire to save face.

The characters in small-town family melodramas may believe in their own authenticity, even if we are encouraged to be sceptical. Indeed, their unawareness of the extent to which they are the product of such social factors as their gender, race, and class is crucial to the genre's capacity to be ironic at the characters' expense, although such social determinants are the source of the genre's equally important capacity to forgive them, replacing the characters' tendency to blame themselves and each other by a much broader ideological critique. So the onstage/offstage opposition as a defining structure of small-town family melodrama is not quite accurate. Nevertheless, a version of it which maintains some of its force while managing without the dubious concept of authenticity is still useful: more specifically, the opposition between the public and the private, each comprising a sort of stage on which a range of performances takes place. In a private moment in Douglas Sirk's 1958 film, *Imitation of Life*, Susie (Sandra Dee) tells her mother Lora (Lana Turner), 'Oh, mama, stop acting!' This can now be seen as an impossible demand for characters who, in some sense, are always on stage.

Scandals and alibis

Despite the fact that any physical space can function as a dramaturgical stage, many films use theatres, actors, and performances within their narrative worlds to give greater prominence to such concerns and to stand as a metaphor for the wider narrative world. Our first sustained example, Douglas Sirk's *All I Desire* (1953), begins with a shot of the Bijou Theatre, from which we dissolve to the showbill displayed out front, and then to Naomi Murdoch (Barbara Stanwyck) backstage, on her way to the dressing room she shares with an older performer named Belle (Lela Bliss). We see

41

FIGURE 8 *Naomi at the Bijou Theatre*

nothing of the show itself, although Naomi is clearly disappointed in a career going nowhere fast. Belle hands her a letter from Naomi's younger daughter Lily (Lori Nelson), inviting her mother back home for her high school graduation, and we learn that Naomi abandoned her three children and husband Henry (Richard Carlson) in the small town of Riverdale, Wisconsin, many years before.

The film is a useful example for several reasons. We are immediately shown the various forms of acting and pretence in Naomi's life. As a vaudeville performer she is almost at the bottom of the bill and at the end of her rope, as she tells us in voice-over at the beginning of the film, although Belle says she is too classy for this place and should return to the legitimate theatre. Her children, on the other hand, think she is in Europe doing Shakespeare: as Naomi tells Belle, 'That's my story and I'm stuck with it'. Finally, she is a mother who has abandoned her family and yet is longing to go back. So it is impossible to point with certainty to any one of these incompatible roles as more 'real' or 'authentic' than any other. Although Belle describes Naomi as inherently classy, despite her present circumstances, Naomi sees her status as a legitimate actress as no more than a made-up story with no factual basis, the film thereby setting up a contrast between essentialist and experiential definitions of the self (a contrast, that is, between the idea that we each have an unchanging essence which remains no matter how our situation may change, and the idea that we become whatever our circumstances make us). The brave face Naomi puts on as Belle reads the letter out loud is undermined by the way we see her as a reflection in the mirror as she repeats her earlier, clearly false dismissal of the letter: 'I told you it was a laugh'. At the end of the scene, when she has decided to go home, Belle's advice – 'Let your hair go back to natural, act real classy. Why, you'd be their idea of a perfect lady and a big star' – emphasises that, at home as well, she will be playing a part. After all, as Naomi herself concedes, as she begins to take the idea more seriously, 'I've done it on the stage'.

The other important aspect of the scene, in terms of the recurring concerns of small-town family melodrama, is the introduction of the idea of scandal. The first hint of its thematic importance is when Naomi tells us in her opening voice-over that, with summer coming, the air is even staler than usual in the broken-down theatres to which she is now reduced: 'Brother, there's not much to look forward to. Well, I guess some people might say maybe I asked for it.' As we listen to her voice, we see her walking through the backstage clutter and down a flight of stairs, the male performer on stage seen only as a dancing shadow through the screen that serves as a backdrop behind him. Naomi is shown from above and through the banisters as she goes down the stairs, the camera then cutting to a position below her as she continues down and ducks her head under a sort of horizontal pipe intervening between her and us, an effect repeated in the dressing room where a high-angle shot shows a wooden beam partially blocking her from view as she enters.

In the course of the conversation with Belle, Naomi tells her that Henry always said she would end up disgracing him and the kids. When Belle asks whether this was due to another man, Naomi replies, 'I pulled out before there was a scandal'. However, when Naomi later returns home, her husband remarks critically: 'Our lives are settled now. We've lived down the talk, the ... the scandal.' So was there a scandal, as he maintains, or was there not, as she insists? Naomi's and Henry's accounts are compatible only if we assume two separate scandals, one a potential scandal only, the second scandal alone made fully public: Naomi pulled out before there was a widespread revelation of her adulterous relationship with Dutch Heineman (Lyle Bettger), but she thereby left Henry with a full-blown scandal in her abandonment of the children and him. Naomi's secret affair, although known to some of the townsfolk, turns out to be no more scandalous than her open desire for independence and a career. Therefore, although she implies to Belle that she left town not from a positive desire to have a career on the stage, but from a self-sacrificing desire to spare her family any more trouble, this is not completely convincing, although her attributing to others the view that she is scandalous certainly suggests that she is not completely willing to take on the full burden of blame.

To some extent she looks the sort of woman who would shock and titillate a Midwestern small town. Her costume is scanty and over-decorated, with a feather trailing from the tight blonde curls on her head, her shoulders bare, and the bodice closely fitting and festooned with drapery below the waist. And yet there is a whiff of humiliation about such a costume on a woman who is clearly approaching middle-age (Stanwyck herself in her mid-forties at the time). Belle, who is even older, takes a motherly interest in Naomi, significantly reminding her that, in the legitimate theatre, 'There's real prestige ... you don't have to worry about getting old,' and there is a pervading sense of disappointment and disillusionment in the conversation between them. Both come across as mature and sympathetic women making do in a world which no longer appreciates them and in which time is their enemy. It is ironically appropriate that, when Naomi ends up staying in Riverdale longer than she had intended, it is because Lily has moved the clock back, causing her mother to miss her train.

As Naomi's description of Riverdale overlaps with our first view of the town, we see her older daughter Joyce (Marcia Henderson) being helped out of a horse-drawn buggy by her fiancé Russ (Richard Long). Her outfit

FIGURE 9 *Joyce in Riverdale*

and appearance could hardly be more different from Naomi's in the previous scene: she is covered up to the neck in a modest dress, her dark hair pulled back severely beneath a flat and unattractive hat, and her prim appearance and disapproving manner combine to make her look somewhat older than she is. Thus, like her mother, she appears to be playing a role to which she is not completely matched. Further, in spite of the contrasting costumes between mother and daughter, the bare white skin of Naomi's shoulders and upper body above the bodice is echoed by the plain white fabric of the sailor collar which covers the same parts of Joyce, while the dark stripes around the high neck of Joyce's dress recall the necklace tightly fastened around her mother's neck, producing a similar effect of constraint. Russ's quip as he steals a kiss – 'Shall we scandalise the neighbours?' – provides a further link between Naomi and Joyce. Of course the 'scandal' of Russ kissing Joyce is much more innocent than her mother's transgressions. What their actions share in terms of scandal, however, is that each is an inappropriate acting out of a private performance upon a public stage: a public display of private family dramas and relationships for the whole town to see.

So scandal is the result of inappropriate public displays of private concerns, and its opposite – where public displays of family dramas and relationships are seen to be appropriate (weddings, funerals, and so on) – is ritual. Ritual and scandal are the two poles of small-town family melodramas which respectively regulate and disrupt the traffic between private and public spaces so central to the genre's interests. Thus public kisses are perfectly acceptable in the context of a wedding, say, and may even form part of the ritual itself (as when a groom is told, 'You may kiss the bride'), and are only mildly transgressive, if at all, in the case of Russ and Joyce, who are engaged to be married. It is not kisses themselves which are scandalous, but the secrets they reveal. The past love affair between Naomi and Dutch – a case of unregulated female desire – is shocking because it is symptomatic of the deeper scandal that her husband has lost control of his wife, as indeed is the fact that she abandons him to go on the stage and display herself publicly to other men. The sexual desirability and desirousness of women may not be inappropriate in themselves, but may indicate a deeper 'problem' of domestic disorder and male powerlessness within the domestic space. This is one of several key scandals for which other, milder scandals may be no more than alibis or screens.

The world of small-town family melodrama is one in which hierarchical structures based on gender, race, and class are firmly entrenched, and the relative power of white men of the middle- and upper-classes over others who are either female, black, or lower-class is generally seen as right and proper by the characters within this world, even those who are poorly served by such beliefs. So it is not only when women attempt to take on the prerogatives of men that scandal is produced. For example, in another film directed by Douglas Sirk, *Imitation of Life*, Sarah Jane Johnson (Susan Kohner), whose mother Annie (Juanita Moore) is black but who is herself light-skinned, is passing as white in order to avoid the prejudice and discrimination which would otherwise come her way. When Sarah Jane leaves home to escape her mother's well-intentioned interference, Annie keeps on turning up as living proof that her daughter has stepped outside her 'proper' place. When Annie leaves the privacy of the home where she works as a maid, and enters the public arena of night-clubs and cheap hotels where Sarah Jane works and lives, the potential scandal she trails is displayed in her body itself. As with *All I Desire*, where Naomi's body as a performer in vaudeville was not scandalous in itself, but only when juxtaposed with the family she has left behind, so too is Annie's blackness only a cause for scandal when juxtaposed with her daughter, who is trying to make it as white.

The two examples are not precisely equivalent. Although Sarah Jane and Naomi are both transgressive, in refusing to accept their subordinate position, it is Annie who keeps turning up to disabuse those who have accepted Sarah Jane as white, whereas it is Naomi herself whose turning up in Riverdale produces scandal for her family who have painstakingly repaired their respectable façade in the years she's been away. However, in both cases it is the undermining of a character's or a family's position in the social hierarchy, a position achieved through the presentation of what is seen as a false front, which is in play. It is because of the precariousness of such a front that Joyce's puritanical manner appears to be so exaggerated, as if its excess is a defensive reaction to her knowledge of how easily the whole thing could come tumbling down. Similarly, the version of whiteness which Sarah Jane takes on is a distastefully racist one, again an exaggerated defence against the threat of her mother's reappearance.

This is worth exploring more closely. On the one hand, we need to distinguish those who are scandalous – through overstepping their position within social hierarchies – from those whose bodies bear the marks of scandal even though they may be innocent of 'bad' behaviour themselves. However, the two may often coexist in one and the same person: for example, the body of a woman who has a scandalous affair may bear its marks if she becomes visibly pregnant. On the other hand, we must differentiate between those who are scandalised and those who, while neither thrilled nor offended by the scandal, may still try to cover it up or to repair the rifts it has caused, whether out of embarrassment, pain, or more dispassionate self-interest, or at least a belief that their interests are being served by an appearance of respectability. Here, too, it is possible for a character to be both: Sarah Jane's boyfriend Frankie (Troy Donahue), in *Imitation of Life*, who beats her up when he finds out that her mother is black, is a good example, his horror equalled only by the compensating violence he metes out. More commonly, the scandalised are bystanders to the main events, which unfold like a particularly salacious melodrama for them to enjoy and ostentatiously deplore.

Naomi tells Henry, 'Well, I'm not the girl from across the tracks who used to embarrass you, not anymore. I won't laugh too loud or make jokes or speak to the riffraff I knew before I married you,' but despite her best efforts to act 'classy', as Belle advised, her reappearance in the town as an attractive and vivacious woman is enough to start the tongues wagging, perhaps as much from memories of her vulgar origins as of the circumstances of her departure years ago. Henry's efforts to repair the damage consist, above all, in the careful presentation of the family as a united front when they all attend Lily's school play together, the audience having swollen to include what seems like the whole town, all considerably more eager to watch Naomi than the pupils onstage. However, when Dutch tries to force himself on Naomi a couple of days later, and she accidentally injures him when his gun goes off, his damaged body takes over as the visible manifestation of their scandalous relationship.

The crowds are quick to gather outside the doctor's office, assuming wrongly that the shooting was deliberate, and taking malicious pleasure in their communication of the news – 'She shot Dutch Heineman' – while the doctor himself advises Naomi to leave town because of the gossip which the shooting is sure to generate as soon as he makes his report to the police. The prurient interest in Dutch's injury may reveal the townsfolk's fascination with their past affair, although it is less easy to see how her shooting him would be compatible with a resumption of the affair in the present. However, a woman shooting a man may also be seen as an overstepping of a woman's role in its own right, whether or not a past affair is implied, and thereby might be thought of as scandalous in itself. Nevertheless, Henry is able to accept this transgression once Dutch helps him to see it as a defence of the family: 'Now I suppose she's spreading it around town she had to plug me to stop me from going after her.' In this sense, the shooting becomes redeemable as another form of exaggerated reaction to external attempts to breach the family's defences, like Joyce's puritanical manner and the presentation of the family as a united front at Lily's play.

In *Imitation of Life* Sarah Jane is the transgressor, while Annie is an innocent bearer of the marks of Sarah Jane's transgression as a genetically 'black' person trying to be white. However, the night-club owner who fires Sarah Jane as soon as her mother turns up is not so much scandalised as self-interestedly attuned to the racism of the marketplace he serves, in which he offers beautiful (white) women to a leering clientele. In any case, he inhabits the city, not the town, and scandal has little purchase here. The only character we see being scandalised by revelations about Sarah Jane's racial background is her white boyfriend Frankie, who viciously beats her as a result. Although the film is set in New York rather than in a small town, the family with whom Annie and Sarah Jane live have moved to the suburbs by then, so the same small-town dynamic is at work in her relationship with Frankie, before she runs away.

One more example may be useful before we move on to examine some of the strategies used by those who, while neither scandalous nor scandalised themselves, are actively engaged in saving face. Richard Fleischer's *Mandingo* (1975), set in the declining years of slavery in the American South, is somewhat later than the other films examined in this book, and therefore shows how the structures we have been looking at persist across any ostensible classical/postclassical divide. The most obvious scandal is the sexual relationship between the Mandingo slave Mede (Ken Norton) and Blanche (Susan George), wife of Hammond Maxwell (Perry King), a slave-owner who lives with his father Warren (James Mason) on a large slave-breeding plantation. Although there are extenuating circumstances for both Blanche and Mede, and the film extends considerable sympathy, rather than blame, to them both, it remains the case that, in terms of the organising structures of scandal, they have each overstepped their positions as Hammond's wife and slave respectively. When their baby is born, the colour of his body announces their transgression. Yet, since the birth occurs in the privacy of the Maxwell home, it never quite goes public to become a full-blown scandal. The attending doctor and his wife express concern and dismay, rather than horror, and Hammond's father seems more worried and regretful than shocked at the birth, going so far as to defend Blanche in order to forestall his son's reaction. Even in front of such a small and private audience, Hammond's humiliation is so deep as to require an extraordinarily excessive amount of 'repair work' to bury all traces of the event: Blanche, Mede and the baby must all be killed, in a collusive series of actions involving Hammond, his father, the doctor and his wife, all collectively groping for a way out of their perplexity, the implications of Blanche's relationship with Mede beyond their powers to untangle and fully comprehend. As they try to set Hammond's reputation to rights upon the public stage – by massive repression behind the scenes – they seem like bewildered figures acting out the requirements of an ideology which controls them without their knowledge and full emotional involvement, the participants hardly knowing what to feel. This is reminiscent of the famous metaphor of the cave, in Book VII of Plato's *Republic*, whose chained inhabitants see flickering images cast on the wall by firelight and imagine they are seeing the substance of the world rather than a false representation. This is a metaphor upon which Sirk too seems to draw near the beginning of *All I Desire*, in the dancing figure on the vaudeville stage who is seen only as a shadow from behind the back-cloth, a striking image of a shrouded world.

So Blanche's infidelity stops short of scandal and is excessively suppressed before it has a chance to reveal itself in public. In contrast, the film's main scandal is both public and unrecuperable in its consequences for the white slave-owning élite: the slave rebellion led by Cicero (Ji-Tu Cumbuka) more or less midway through the film. Cicero is singled out for our notice in the first scene in the film, when a line of Warren Maxwell's slaves are lined up and inspected by an unattractive and vulgar prospective buyer. In one of the film's many 'backstage' shots, which give us access to the thoughts and emotions of the slaves beyond the fronts they are compelled to present to their owners from motives of self-preservation, the camera is positioned so that we see the resentment on Cicero's face as the

FIGURE 10 *Cicero 'backstage'*

slave-trader, Brownlee (Paul Benedict), discusses him with Maxwell. When Brownlee throws a stick and orders Cicero to 'Go fetch,' Cicero's carefully measured hesitation before he obeys, and the controlled aggression with which he flings the stick at Brownlee's feet are the extent of the resistance he can offer at this point: just enough to preserve his self-respect, yet not so much as to give Brownlee a sufficiently open display of rebellion to justify a punitive response.

The slave uprising directly follows a scene in which Hammond is in bed with Ellen (Brenda Sykes), the slave who is pregnant with his child, and agrees that, if the child is a boy, he can go free. As Andrew Britton puts it, 'It is as if, by acceding to Ellen's demand, Ham has released the forces that threaten the order of which he is a part' (1976: 19). The news of the slave uprising is accompanied by views of the bodies of a murdered white family laid out on the grass. So, although the prospect of Hammond's mixed-race child is not scandalous in the way that Blanche's child with Mede clearly is (since Hammond's relationship with Ellen is perfectly acceptable in polite plantation society, posing no challenge to his position as a dominant white male), nonetheless the concession to Ellen that her child can go free leads directly to the display of dead white bodies which are evidence of a violent appropriation of freedom by Cicero and the other rebelling slaves. Just as Blanche's baby, which is 'supposed' to be white, turns out to be black, so these white bodies, which are 'supposed' to be powerful, turn out to be dead.

The answering violence of the retribution meted out to the transgressive slaves, like Frankie's beating up of Sarah Jane in *Imitation of Life*, goes beyond the 'repair work' carried out in cases where the presentation of an intact façade is still a possibility. Indeed, even in the case of Blanche's relationship with Mede, although the murder of their baby may possibly preserve the fiction of a marriage where Hammond is still in charge, the subsequent murders of Blanche and Mede escalate the process to such an extent that it becomes counter-productive and indistinguishable from mere revenge. Where damaged reputations can no longer be restored by plastering over the cracks in faulty relationships or where a continuing threat remains, cosmetic repair is thus replaced by aggressive repudiation or destruction of the usurpers. One of the terrible ironies in *Mandingo* is that Mede is made the instrument of Cicero's capture and thus of his death, realising too late that his loyalty to Hammond is incompatible with his links to Cicero as a fellow slave whose interests he shares. However, there are a number of recuperative strategies for dealing with scandal by those it besmirches which fall short of such violent extremes and which we will now examine, as they are prevalent across a broad range of small-town films.

Saving face

The initial question raised about the difference between being onstage or offstage, and the subsequent reformulation of this in terms of being on a public stage or on a private stage, has led us to the centrality of scandal as a thematic preoccupation of small-town family melodramas. The kinds of secrets which emerge as scandal when they are inappropriately displayed in public have been seen to circle around the transgressions of those members of subordinate groups who step outside of their ideologically designated roles: women trying to make it in a man's world or seeking sexual partners beyond the marriage bed, black people trying to pass as white, slaves killing white masters, and so on.

It may be helpful to contrast such films with those of genres where different sorts of secrets prevail. Crime films provide an example of what seems to be a very different dynamic at work. The protagonists of crime films are less concerned with preserving a respectable appearance and more interested in keeping out of jail and getting away with their crimes. As long as nothing can be proven against them, they can generally live with a tarnished reputation. Similarly, the anonymity of the crime film's typically urban setting is one where corruption is so ingrained and indifference to it so pervasive that it is more difficult for scandal to take hold. Thus, in *Party Girl*, we saw how Tommy Farrell's bad reputation as a lawyer for the mob was widely known and how his lack of family life meant he had little to lose from this, at least until the relationship with Vicky produced a need for her respect (although this was not a matter of presenting her with a false front of respectability, but of openly repudiating his past and going straight with her support). His willingness to court death in order to guarantee her safety is evidence of a more genuine strength and integrity than men susceptible to scandal are likely to possess. This is particularly the case in film noir, where the male protagonist in urban crime films may be ambivalently poised between desires to be strong and tough and equally powerful desires to let go (see Thomas 1992b), so Tommy's courage may have a suicidal edge to it as well – a tiredness and defeatism in the face of such a bleak and dirty world – which Vicky's positive presentation as a figure of salvation for him may only just stave off. Indeed, it is not just the look and structure of *Party Girl*, but also the depth and mutual commitment of their relationship, which is most crucial in differentiating the film from its noir relations.

In some cases, particularly those where the protagonist of a film noir is a respectable married man who has fallen into adultery as well as crime, the film may have aspects of small-town family melodrama as well – the two genres are far from completely distinct – athough his attitude to the secret he conceals may include not so much a fear of scandal as a fear of punishment, yet at the same time a desire for punishment and, through it, for release from marriage as well. Thus, in Fritz Lang's *Woman in the Window* (1944), if Richard Wanley (Edward G. Robinson) reveals his unconscious desires in the dream which constitutes the main part of the film, it is a dream not just of near infidelity and crime but of excessive punishment to the point of suicide. With his wife away and his male friends jokingly egging him on to infidelity, it seems unlikely that the revelation of his near-adultery (which stops well short of consummation) would cause much of a stir, especially given the New York setting and the absence of small-town gossip. Yet he conspires to murder a blackmailer rather than admit to a justified killing in self-defence which would bring the relatively slight sexual lapse to public notice, thereby setting himself on a course of self-destruction which hovers between regretful defeatism and wilful surrender. Film noir centres upon the difficulties involved in being a tough guy, and the unacknowledged desire to stop trying, and death is often the final result. The more melodramatic examples of film noir whose protagonists are transgressive married men may include a concern with the difficulties involved in being respectable as well, and the temptation to stray.

In small-town family melodramas, however, the threats to male respectability are less likely to derive from the men themselves, but from the women who undermine them at home and whose behaviour is in danger of broadcasting this state of affairs to the world, which is to say the town. Such men are intent on preserving the appearance of being in control, no matter how disempowered and inadequate they may feel behind the closed doors of the family home. This could not be more dramatically illustrated than in Sam Wood's *Kings Row* (1942). If we try to get our bearings by sorting out who is scandalous, who is scandalised, who is most involved in saving face, and so on, in accordance with our scheme, it soon becomes clear that the town's transgressive women are tightly controlled and kept behind closed doors by the town's leading lights: in other words, the recuperative efforts of those men who have most to lose if the various scandals were to emerge have been largely successful, but only at the expense of these women.

Thus, Dr Tower (Claude Rains) keeps his 'mad' wife inside the house away from contact with anyone outside the family, visible only as a solitary figure at the window upstairs, and when his daughter Cassandra (played as a child by Mary Thomas) gets upset because of the poor turnout at her birthday party, he withdraws her from school and keeps her confined to the house, like her mother before her. He thus takes her perfectly under-standable display of emotion as the first sign of an inherited mental ill-ness, although her strange behaviour later in the film, after years of isola-tion, is just as likely to have resulted from her father's treatment as from an innately disordered mind. Similarly, Dr Gordon (Charles Coburn), with the complicity of his wife, refuses to let his daughter Louise (Nancy Coleman) go out with Drake McHugh (Ronald Reagan) and, when she later threatens to tell the whole town about the unnecessary punitive operations he has performed on those of whom he disapproves, including Drake, he counters by threatening to commit her to a mental asylum, upping the stakes in the battle between them. Both doctors see female emotion – or what Dr Gordon refers to in Louise's case as her 'making a spectacle of herself' – as a cause for concern. The more these women are kept inside, the more exag-gerated their expressions of emotion become, and the more violent are the efforts to control and restrain them, in an unending vicious circle.

Dr Tower also escalates the scale of his control over his daughter when he kills her and then himself, although it is not clear precisely what moti-vates this switch from 'repair work' to something more like the violent ret-ribution seen earlier in the discussions of *Mandingo* and *Imitation of Life*, although some sort of failure in his control over Cassie (Betty Field) seems to be involved. Parris (Robert Cummings), Cassie's childhood sweetheart, who has become Dr Tower's student, concludes from Tower's journal that he killed Cassie to spare Parris the sort of life he himself has endured with a mad wife and a dead-end career hidden away in the inconsequential small town of Kings Row. However, Cassie's plea to Parris to take her away – and his refusal – implicates Parris in the process of her containment within the home and town. Shortly after Cassie's desperate outburst, Parris and Drake secretly watch her opening the door to the porch of her house, where her father is quietly sitting on the swing smoking, his head hidden in the shadows, and they are convinced by this appearance of domestic calm that all is well. As Dr Tower follows his daughter inside, the swing continues to creak as it moves back and forth after his exit, a chilling prelude to murder and suicide.

It may be that Dr Tower's motives are more to do with his own despair, with Cassie as a casualty of his suicidal desires, as he seems to imply in an earlier conversation with Parris about the ills of the modern world where, in Tower's words, 'man breaks down under the strain, the bewilderment, disappointment and disillusionment, gets lost, goes crazy, commits suicide'. However, Parris replies by suggesting that people need to get fooled back into reality when they have lost their way, and that it is 'like catching a rabbit straight out of its pen. You get his attention on something else and he doesn't see the gate, and first thing he knows, he's back home again'. Tower commends Parris for the phrase 'back home again in the pen', and tells him approvingly that if he had a son, he would want him to be just like Parris.

If Dr Tower fails to acknowledge the way his description of the ills of the modern world applies to himself as much as to his daughter, so too is Parris oblivious to the links between his views of effecting a psychiatric cure by returning people to their 'pens' and Cassie's imprisonment within the home and her subsequent death, not to mention the callous way he is prepared to contemplate committing Louise to an institution after her father's death in order to protect Drake from hearing some painful truths. If he expects Louise to put herself entirely in his hands, he insists to Drake's wife Randy (Ann Sheridan) in contrast that, in Drake's case, 'the helpless invalid complex must be avoided at all cost'. It is clear that for all three doctors – Gordon, Tower, and Parris himself – women are the ones who most need to be securely confined within the home or the asylum or, failing that, the grave.

Significantly, Parris' diagnosis of what Drake needs – and his willingness, in his own words, to condemn Louise to 'a life of unspeakable horror' in order to give it to him – is mistaken, and it is the nineteen-year-old Elise

FIGURE 11 *Parris coming up against the camera*

(Kaaren Verne), who now lives in what was once his house, who sets him on the right track. He now tells Drake the truth about his needless surgery, and sets Louise loose to broadcast her father's misdeeds to anyone she likes. Parris tells Elise that his return to the house he shared with his grandmother is 'like coming home', and it is clear that 'home' represents something much more positive to him than to either Cassie or Louise, his grandmother, at the opposite extreme to those women who refuse to accept their place in a man's world or to those men who impose their wills on their children through punishment and constraint.

However, despite the happiness of Parris' early years, the depiction of childhood in Kings Row is generally bleak. Not only do we see young Cassie in tears at Louise's meanness in holding a party on the same day as Cassie's and poaching most of her guests, but later that day we see another child crying in despair as Dr Gordon operates on his father without an anaesthetic. Even in the earlier scene of Parris and Cassie swimming together in the pond – a memory he clearly treasures – the children are filmed half-obscured by dark hanging tendrils from the surrounding trees, and the adult Parris tells Elise 'we were just babies but I think we knew we ought not to,' so that what should have been an innocent idyll is already undermined by guilt and an oppressive natural setting.

Indeed, nature generally provides a dark running commentary throughout the film: most obviously in the storm that accompanies the beginnings of Parris' sexual relationship with Cassie, but also in the frozen wintry weather throughout the early days of Parris' apprenticeship with Dr Tower, an apprenticeship which increasingly implicates Parris in a doctrine requiring the containment and control of female passion, so that the ice and snow associated with Parris' increasing alignment with Dr Tower contrasts with the stormy weather associated with his relationship with Cassandra. The film's least transgressive woman is Parris' grandmother, and Elise seems set to follow in her footsteps, linked to her by both her European background and her association with his childhood home, which suggests that she will embody a similar self-sacrificing love for Parris at the expense of any passionate desires of her own.

In the previous chapter we saw how *My Darling Clementine's* visual juxtaposition of Clementine Carter with a pot of water bubbling away on the stove served to remind us of the strength of her feelings underneath her self-contained façade. There is a comparable moment in *Kings Row* when Parris and his grandmother are talking, Parris with a window at his back through which we see the snow swirling down, while his grandmother is seated by the fireplace, whose lively flames give some indication, perhaps, of what the years of self-sacrifice have suppressed. It is tempting to see her terminal illness as a manifestation of her body's rebellion after so many years of sacrifice and self-denial, although this is clearly a rebellion that has nowhere positive to go.

Even Randy, an energetic character whose presentation is largely positive, speaks of how her feelings for Drake have changed since Dr Gordon amputated his legs unnecessarily: 'I knew then that I didn't love him any less, only differently, with an overwhelming new calm feeling … that so completely took the place of the old excitement'. Randy too has been 'calmed down' in the journey from tomboy child to adult to wife, although a passing remark she makes in childhood – 'It's a free world … I guess' – shows some awareness, in the qualifying doubt she adds at the end, of what may lie ahead. Parris, too, is a sympathetic character, despite his ideological links with the film's most monstrous men and, like the characters in *Mandingo* who are baffled by the ideological conundrum of what to do with Blanche's baby, he is bewildered by the world around him and caught up in ways of thinking whose implications he can barely see.

This is conveyed most forcefully just after the young Cassie tells him her father is removing her from school. The scene – and the childhood sequence as a whole – ends with Parris (played as a child by Scotty Beckett) moving forward, as Cassie walks away offscreen. As Parris approaches the camera, the film cuts to a shot of him uncomfortably close to the lens, before he turns and walks away. Given that, as a fictional character, he has no knowledge of being in a film, the effect is as if he is suddenly brought up against an invisible barrier which stops him in his tracks, a barrier whose existence he senses rather than perceives. The moment provides a visual equivalent for the way that ideological constraints are felt, but not consciously acknowledged, by the inhabitants of Kings Row, qualifying Parris' freedom in the same way as Randy's 'I guess' in the above quotation qualifies hers.

Minnelli's *Some Came Running* (1958) provides a further example of a man returning home to the town he had tried to escape. However, whereas Parris' return is prompted by the need to help Drake, the return of writer Dave Hirsh (Frank Sinatra) is inadvertent: his army pals deposited him on the bus when he was drunk, and he wakes to find himself in his home town of Parkman, Indiana. Yet the facts that he had told his buddies the name of the town and that he arrives in Parkman while asleep combine to produce an impression that his return enacts an unconscious wish, perhaps a need to clear up unfinished business from years before. His brother Frank (Arthur Kennedy), who had rejected him when he was a boy, is susceptible to scandal on several fronts: his wife Agnes (Leora Dana) humiliates him at home and Dave embarrasses him in public in a variety of ways, from putting his money in a rival bank to the one on whose board Frank sits to getting into fights and hanging out with unsuitable friends. Frank and Agnes' conversations are laced with anxieties about what people will think or say, with Agnes still smarting from Dave's thinly disguised exposure of her in a novel he wrote.

Like Parris in *Kings Row*, Dave ends up as an enforcer of the town's repressive regime, particularly with respect to his brother and his niece, both of whom he 'saves' from unsuitable relationships, and again some of Parkman's women are complicit in their own confinement within the town and home, although with much more resentment and mean spirit than Parris' grandmother and his future wife ever show. So *Some Came Running* shares the face-saving strategy of staving off or repairing scandal by putting women in their place (both physically, within the home and town, and more generally, within supportive and subordinate roles). It is difficult to say which film is more pessimistic. Parris at least ends up by setting Louise free to destroy her father's reputation throughout the town, whereas Dave Hirsh is unredeemably nasty, his future relationship with Gwen French (Martha Hyer) set to become a carbon copy of the destructive relationship between Frank and Agnes. However, a more hopeful aspect of *Some Came Running* is that Frank's secretary, Edith Barclay (Nancy Gates), and his daughter Dawn (Betty Lou Keim) escape from Parkman near the end of the film, with the possibility of becoming friends as they head out of town together on the bus. The film's narrative – in which Dave comes home but Edith and Dawn get away – holds out some hope of female solidarity and escape for two of the film's more sympathetic women.

Nevertheless, the film ends with a funeral which is a study in hypocrisy as Dave, his gambler friend Bama (Dean Martin) and Gwen all pay their final respects to Ginny Moorhead (Shirley MacLaine), having treated her with nothing but disdain when she was alive. The only other people at the funeral are a group of women – presumably Ginny's lower-class friends from work – who stand slightly apart under some trees, their faces obscured by shadows. The funeral functions to obscure Ginny's transgressive image as well, through her literal burial (just as Annie's blackness in *Imitation of Life* is finally hidden away in a coffin covered by white flowers at the funeral which ends that film). Like Naomi Murdoch at the start of *All I Desire*, Ginny looks the part of a disreputable woman when she first arrives in town: she is garishly over-dressed, wearing cheap jewellery and too much make-up, although her wide-eyed enthusiasm and childish manner have little in common with Naomi's intelligence and cynical worldliness. Unlike Naomi, Ginny is young and naïve, expressing her feelings openly, with only a scant understanding of just how badly she is being used, and with none of Naomi's skills at remaking herself as a 'lady'.

Both Dave and Gwen exploit their professional skill with words in heartless put-downs at her expense, for example when Ginny declares her admiration for Gwen, adding, 'I've got nothing, not even a reputation,' and Gwen replies cruelly, 'I'm sure you have a reputation, Miss Moorhead', or when Dave condescendingly wishes her luck with her new 'career' at the local brassiere factory. The chain of events which leads to Ginny's death involves both Gwen and Dave using Ginny as a pawn in their own conflicted relationship, culminating in Dave marrying Ginny to get back at Gwen. When, finally, the drunk and jealous Raymond (Stephen Peck) comes gunning for Dave, and Ginny puts herself in the way, the responsibility for her death is widely shared, even if only Raymond pulls the trigger.

Frank's relationship with Agnes, and Dave's with Gwen, are the only sort the town seems able to absorb, where ambitious women and unhappy men chase public prestige at the expense of emotional warmth. In such a context, Frank's choice of Edith and Dave's choice of Ginny as respective alternatives to Agnes and Gwen, provide each man with a temporary chance to regain self-esteem through a relationship with a woman who is clearly beneath them in class, and thus more easily governable and pliant in response to the men's desires. Such 'slumming' is another strategy for saving face when the control and containment of the more respectable women falls short. Hammond's love for the slave Ellen, in *Mandingo*, achieves similar ends, in contrast to his difficulties in managing his wife Blanche, and there are plenty of additional examples of films where men choose weak or lower-class women as alternatives to more powerful, classier ones: Alfred Hitchcock's *Rebecca* (1940), Ida Lupino's *The Bigamist* (1953), Vincente Minnelli's *Home From the Hill* (1960), and so on.

This is quite different from what happens in film noir, whose men are often drawn to women of obvious sexual power or wealth. As Michael Wood puts it, such films 'were all about greed ... about wanting to climb into the class of the idle rich' (1975: 101–2). The men in small-town family melodramas may be more modest in their choices – or, at least, they may compensate for conventional choices made for the sake of appearances by choosing alternative women to bolster their sense of control when it has been undermined by their more respectable partners. This dynamic is also different from cases where women go shopping for lower-class men, for example Marylee (Dorothy Malone) in Douglas Sirk's *Written on the Wind* (1956), who explains that the wrong end of town 'can be exciting', as well as Blanche in *Mandingo*, who forces Mede into her bed. Both of these women act out of frustrated desires for respectable men, and not from a desire to dominate – and be seen to do so – which characterises their male equivalents, although the distinction is not absolute, since women too may seek a degree of control and men can react to sexual frustration at home, as Wade (Robert Mitchum) does in *Home From the Hill*, and, indeed, this is an aspect of Frank Hirsh's behaviour in *Some Came Running* as well. Nevertheless, a difference in emphasis remains.

Although the relationships of respectable men with women from the wrong side of the tracks are face-saving devices which tend to be indulged in fairly openly, they become an embarrassment or worse if such men and women marry or have a child. The death of Ginny in *Some Came Running* is a public spectacle on the small-town stage, against the heightened funfair backdrop of Parkman's centennial celebrations, following the wedding of Ginny and Dave. The style of the sequence – especially the music, colours, and the rhythms of the editing – mimics Raymond's movements and violent mood, rather than Dave's and Ginny's meandering progress as they wander through the crowd. Thus the newly married couple seem out of place as Parkman is transformed into a full-colour version of the film noir city. Ginny's aspirations to a life of respectable domesticity which are emphasised as she kisses a child and as they walk past a woman demonstrating household gadgets are particularly ill-suited to the nightmarish look that increasingly defines the space crowding in around them, as well as to its violent rhythms and sounds.

As Bama rushes through the streets, trying to catch up with Dave before Raymond does, and as Raymond's first gunshot rings out, Ginny and Dave are forced to confront the emotionally volatile and dangerous world which their marriage appears to have called up. In fact, given Dave's lack of enthusiasm for the marriage, as evidenced by his continuing bad temper and condescension towards Ginny, it is easy to see Raymond's drunken attack on the couple as an acting out of Dave's own hostility and self-disgust. A crowd quickly gathers, and Raymond's killing of Ginny reveals itself as yet another example of the sort of excessive violence which is not so much a scandal in itself as a reparation-cum-retribution for the greater scandal of Ginny's stepping outside of her class through the unsuitable marriage to Dave.

So we are back to our starting point, when *It's a Wonderful Life* was seen as offering an example of the doubleness – or even the double doubleness – of the melodramatic small town. The overwhelming sense of a noir city erupting through Parkman's respectable façade provides a parallel to Pottersville emerging out of Bedford Falls, and Bama's cowboy hat may remind us of the western in the way that George Bailey's dreams of lassoing the moon do in Capra's film. Certainly, the links with these genres of male toughness and individuality imply that the small town contains within it alternative versions of itself and fantasies of escape. This is not just a matter of the disempowered refusing to keep to their places, as dramatised by the scenarios of scandal throughout these films, but equally of those with a good name and position within the town dreaming of freedom from respectability itself and from the constant effort of papering over its cracks.

Suggestions for further reading

The literature on melodrama is extensive, both in its narrowly generic sense (for example Gledhill (1987); Cavell (1996)) and as a broader category that cuts across genres (Thomas (2000)). However, the discussion of dramaturgical spaces presented in this chapter can best be understood as an application of the ideas of American sociologist Erving Goffman (1974) to the realm of domestic small-town melodrama, and his contrast between offstage and onstage spaces provides a convenient framework for making sense of scandal as a central generic concern.

3   CINEMATIC SPACES: BACKGROUND AND FOREGROUND, ONSCREEN AND OFFSCREEN

It is time to look closely at the role played by those strategies aimed specifically at us as viewers and inaccessible to the characters within the film. In order to do so, we will concentrate on a single film, Otto Preminger's *Advise and Consent*. It will inevitably prove impossible to isolate such strategies from aspects of the setting and its decor, or to disregard the contrasts between public and private spaces so central to the film's dramatic structures. Nevertheless, the emphasis will be on questions about the nature of Preminger's camera and its relation both to the world it reveals and to the audience it addresses. How can the camerawork be characterised? What sort of things are included in or excluded from the image, and how are they placed relative to the various spatial axes of the frame (more particularly, the left-to-right and top-to-bottom axes which cross the borders of the frame, and the axis which extends from the camera into the depth of the image)? What are the shadings of tone and affect and the degrees of knowledge which the camerawork offers or withholds? And, finally, how do all these decisions serve the thematic interests of the film?

Advise and Consent (Otto Preminger, 1962)

The first image after the credit sequence is carefully composed with a newsboy holding a paper in the right foreground of the shot, the headline clearly visible: 'Leffingwell Picked For Secretary Of State'. The background is nondescript, with trees, a road and a parked car on the left, while the newsboy's short sleeves indicate a sunny day and, at the same time, give an air of casualness to the scene. There is a slight reframing as a man who we later discover to be the Majority Whip, Senator Stanley Danta (Paul Ford), approaches the newsboy to buy a paper, the camera keeping him in frame as he moves right while reading the lead story on the front page. The camera movement reveals the lower portion of an official-looking building in the background with a queue of people along the building's side, although they are small figures behind the foreground figure of Danta, whose surprised reaction has our attention as he hails a cab and gets in. At this point the camera pulls back to reveal the Capitol dome, suddenly turning the anonymous setting and vaguely official-looking building into a very specific and instantly recognisable signifier of the United States government and its institutions of power.

The withholding of this establishing image until the end of the shot is directly relevant to the film's concern with those things which lurk in the backgrounds of the various characters' lives, and with the audience's relationship to such knowledge. The opening scene thus repositions us by a simple camera movement within a single shot – producing an effect something like 'Aha! So that's where we are!' – and alerts us to the importance of camera viewpoint and orientation with respect to the narrative world. It simultaneously offers us a gentle chastisement, perhaps, for our earlier inattention to significant details such as the queue of people outside the building, which signals it as a tourist attraction, in a city which the credit sequence and the newspaper's name have already indicated to be Washington DC. The film's intentions are clear. We will need to pay attention to more than the foreground action, also attending to small details within the narrative world, as well as the shifting relationship between this world and the camera. This is not a film which will deliver its meanings to us on a plate.

As the taxi drives offscreen to the right, we dissolve to a shot of it arriving at its destination, the car approaching the camera from the right background, then edging around a corner so that it continues away from the camera at an oblique angle towards the left rear of the frame. We then cut to a closer shot of the taxi approaching the camera once again, as it pulls to a stop in front of the Sheraton Park Hotel. The complex and shifting relationship of the taxi to the camera viewpoint is a typical and recurring strategy in the film which produces a sense of three-dimensional space independent of the camera's position and control. In particular, the film's representations of its narrative world have considerable spatial depth, the actions within it often located along the background/foreground axis rather than along the horizontal left-right plane.

A further example of such a pattern is to be found as Danta is seen leaving the lift in the hotel, the camera moving to the right to keep him in frame, Danta then turning and continuing down a corridor into the depth of the shot. As we cut to a shot of his entering the suite of Senator Bob Munson (Walter Pidgeon) through a background door, as seen from within the suite, he approaches the camera once more, then turns to the left of the screen until he reaches Munson, who is now included in the shot, on the phone to the President (Franchot Tone). The long takes throughout the film continually keep offscreen space alive as an explicit part of the narrative world by the frequent camera movements and re-framings which reveal what was previously outside the shot and which is subsequently included. This calling up of offscreen space is emphatically dramatised through editing as well, in the rest of the hotel sequence, which is structured around a series of telephone calls where we cut between the people on each end of the line and are thereby introduced to a number of important characters, especially Senator Brigham Anderson (Don Murray), who will prove to be a key figure in the film.

A few observations may be useful here. At one point in Munson's conversation with the President, Munson turns to Danta to pass on what the President has said. The President's immediate response – 'Who's with you?' – underlines both his inability to see what's going on in Munson's room and our own superiority over all three men – Munson, Danta, and the President – in having visual access to both the Presidential office and Munson's suite. However, lest we become over-confident, we too are limited in which bits of which location we are permitted to see, although it is only on a subsequent viewing of the film that this becomes readily apparent. Thus, as the camera moves in on the President when we see him for the first time, he is taking some pills from a bottle as he speaks. When we next cut back to him, he is putting down a water glass. Only when we discover how ill he is in a later scene does his action retrospectively become of sufficient relevance to the narrative for us to realise that a significant event had been withheld from us offscreen, since he presumably takes the pills after the cut back to Munson's room when he is inaccessible to our gaze. Although this is a relatively small event, the onscreen indications of which are unlikely to be noticed on a first viewing, the strategy of its retrospective clarification nevertheless provides a further corrective (like the sudden appearance of the Capitol dome in the opening shot of the film) to any complacent assumptions of epistemological superiority which we may be tempted to make.

Another example of this educative process occurs when Munson's conversation with the President comes to an end and he walks to the right of the screen and then turns and continues into the background of the shot, entering an adjoining room of the suite, then returning towards the camera, turning and walking to our right before exiting offscreen. The pattern of left-to-right movement followed by movement along the background/foreground axis and culminating in an arrival at a door should be familiar by now, and it has the effect, when we cut to a door opening with us outside it, of preparing us for a reappearance of Munson, similar to earlier examples of the pattern (for example, when Danta approached and entered Munson's room), our expectations being that Munson will walk straight towards the camera from what we take to be the door of his suite. Instead, however, a woman exits from what is now seen to be a different suite altogether, that of Senator Lafe Smith (Peter Lawford). As the woman moves to the hotel lift on the right of the screen, Munson and Danta walk from the right to Smith's door on the left, passing by a corridor which leads into the background of the shot. We then cut to the other side of the door as Smith lets them in.

As the series of telephone calls in the hotel sequence are made first thing in the morning, it is unsurprising that most of the participants are drinking coffee as they talk, and such things as coffee pots, cups and saucers are visible in all the inter-cut locations. Still, the sense of work and politics intruding on domesticity is an important theme which escalates in prominence as the sequence proceeds, culminating in Smith's telephone call, at Munson's behest, to Senator Brig Anderson at his home. Although Munson, Danta, and Smith are all seen in impersonal hotel room settings, signalling Munson's situation as a widower and Smith's as a womanising bachelor, and the President is at his desk with the American flag and a framed picture of Lincoln behind him and the Washington Monument visible through one of the windows, ensconced in officialdom rather than domesticity, the process of bringing the political intrusiveness of the calls closer to home begins with the shots of the Minority Leader, Senator Warren Strickland (Will Geer) (whom Munson phones from Smith's suite). Strickland is still in robe and pyjamas and is situated within a much more personalised decor (complete with a rack of guns and a fish on the wall which reinforce his identity as a hunting-and-fishing Republican likely to be opposed to the left-wing Leffingwell). Nevertheless he is alone in the frame whereas, when Munson has Smith phone his friend, Brig Anderson, the domestic and family aspects of the setting are much more abundantly underscored. Here Anderson is on the phone in the left foreground, coffee cup in hand, while his wife Ellen (Inga Swenson) and his young daughter Pidge (Janet Jane Carty) are seated at a table in the garden in the background on the right. The shot presents a picture of idealised family life which should make us suspicious in a film already sufficiently caustic about the omnipresence of backstage manipulations and jockeyings for position and power on the part of the male characters.

The composition of the shot echoes that of its immediate predecessor where, while Smith is on the telephone to Anderson in the left foreground, Munson can be seen as a small figure in an adjoining room of the suite in the far background to the right of the frame. The fact that Munson, as majority leader, is the most commanding figure in the sequence apart from the President himself, suggests once more that small background figures may be extremely powerful narrative forces and that the background presence of Anderson's wife and daughter may similarly carry considerable thematic and narrative weight. The same composition will be repeated later with another image of Brig on the same telephone from the same point of

FIGURE 12 *The ceiling pressing down on Brig*

view, but with one crucial difference: both Ellen and Pidge will be emphatically absent from the shot. The darker implications of the later shot are already prefigured as Ellen brings Pidge in to say goodbye to her father before she leaves for school: as Ellen and Pidge enter and then exit to the left and the camera moves in on Brig, his shadow is visible on the wall behind him as he speaks. This sense of something ominous which 'shadows' or hangs over Brig will be more strongly insisted upon when he is approached by Munson and Senator Tom August (Malcolm Atterbury) in the Capitol building later that day to find out whether he would be willing to chair a Senate subcommittee on Leffingwell's nomination for Secretary of State. For the first time in the film, the ceiling is clearly noticeable in the shot as they talk, producing an oppressive representation of something bearing down on Anderson, which is reinforced as all three men walk off to the rear of the shot, their shadows displayed on the wall to their left.

We are keyed into the first Senate sequence, which follows on from the sequence of telephone calls at the hotel, by a reference to Senator Seabright Cooley (Charles Laughton), followed by a cut to a trolley arriving and 'Seab' getting out, a portly figure in a white suit and dark hat. Seab's path meets that of Munson and Danta as they arrive, and we cut to

Senator Fred Van Ackerman (George Grizzard) emerging into an interior space in the building through a door on the left. As Van Ackerman walks to the right and then turns into a corridor leading towards the back of the frame, Seab passes him in the opposite direction, followed by Munson and Danta, Van Ackerman taking Munson aside to ask to be appointed chair of the subcommittee on Leffingwell, after which Danta and Munson walk off through a door into a suite of offices.

Again and again, the film's carefully choreographed long takes present us with intersecting spaces and crossing paths, with framings and re-framings which mirror the film's political intrigues and its groupings and regroupings as bids for influence and power are made. What is worth noting, however, is that the camerawork, which has such a strong impact in simul-taneously evoking the political and spatial complexities of the narrative world and at the same time clarifying the relationships within it, is almost never put in the service of any one character or position. So Preminger's camera is at once masterly and detached, both a self-conscious and mean-ingful presence and yet remarkably unrhetorical in its refusal to persuade, thus making us aware of the complications of its world while leaving us to draw our own conclusions.

It is difficult to come up with an example from this film of a character who can be understood as wholeheartedly one thing or another in moral terms, since the political realists and manipulators have moments of com-passion and the idealists are flawed. Even Van Ackerman, who is unsympa-thetically portrayed as a humourless left-wing ideologue willing to stoop to blackmail to advance his cause, supports the humane and peace-lov-ing philosophy of Leffingwell, as does Munson, with both Leffingwell and Munson presented as figures of moral weight and humanity (although each has his secrets). On the other hand, both Lafe Smith and the Vice-President (Lew Ayres), who refrain from supporting Leffingwell in the end – as well as Seab, who is vehemently opposed to Leffingwell throughout – are sensitive to Brig Anderson's increasing desperation and offer friendship or a sympa-thetic ear as he edges ever nearer to despair. Decency is not linked to any specific political position, and the film elicits a qualified response from us to virtually all of its characters, yet a response which stops well short of condemnation in most cases. It is not just Van Ackerman's blackmailing of Anderson, but his insistence on seeing everything inflexibly in black and white terms, which excludes him from the generosity of the film's embrace.

The description of Preminger's camera as 'detached' should not be taken to mean 'cold' and 'uncaring', but merely to indicate that its compassionate interest extends across a broad sweep of characters, regardless of political position or power, even those who are in conflict with one another within the narrative itself. Thus, although we are encouraged to take an interest in the political intrigues of the narrative, we are positioned to stand apart from them at the same time. Indeed, the plot's 'hook' – 'Will Leffingwell be approved by the Senate as Secretary of State?' – is a kind of red herring with respect to the film's deeper concerns, although this is not obvious in the early stages of the film.

Our introduction to Robert Leffingwell (Henry Fonda) takes place after Munson asks his secretary to get him on the phone and we cut to Leffingwell's son Johnny (Eddie Hodges), who is seen through the banisters of the staircase as he approaches the ringing phone in the foreground. When we cut to Johnny entering his father's study, the camera moves right to Leffingwell at the typewriter telling Johnny to say he is not home. The sincerity and trustworthiness of Henry Fonda's persona, which feeds into his performance as Leffingwell, as well as the narrative's need for us to see Leffingwell as deserving of the support of Munson, the President and others, are only momentarily unbalanced by such a bare-faced lie. As Leffingwell explains to his son: 'This is a Washington DC kind of lie. That's when the other person knows you're lying and also knows you know he knows.' Leffingwell is not entirely correct in his assumptions, at least as far as Danta is concerned, as Danta's reaction to Munson – 'Wouldn't you think he'd know we'd know he's dodging us?' – amusingly makes clear.

Also worth noting is the way Leffingwell is linked to Brig Anderson through the importance each man gives to his relationship with his child: thus Anderson readily interrupts the phone call from Smith to give Pidge a hug and say goodbye to her as she leaves for school, and Leffingwell is truthful with his son at the same time as he offers expeditious lies to

FIGURE 13 *Dolly's view of the Senate*

his fellow politicians, each man doing his best to separate the world of politics from that of home. The film's interest in such conflicting loyalties and in multi-layered structures of knowledge and supposition continues to accompany the unfolding political intricacies of the plot.

From the scene at Leffingwell's home, the film dissolves to the Senate, where most of the remaining characters will be introduced, and those whom we have already seen engaged in power-plays and intrigues behind the scenes will take their places on a much more public stage. The presentation of the Senate as a place of performance and spectatorship is established from the beginning of the scene as a group of tourists climb the stairs on a guided tour while, in the same long take, the camera's movement to the right reveals Dolly Harrison (Gene Tierney) and two women friends arriving from the background of the shot to take their places in the public gallery above the Senate floor. As we begin to take an interest in Dolly and her friends, the tour guide's words offscreen – 'And in this painting it's interesting to note that Lieutenant Lee and Lieutenant Grant fought side by side' – remind us that political enemies in one context may be allies in another.

The cut to the three women entering the gallery of the Senate initiates a camera movement which begins with them positioned by the door in the back wall of the gallery and facing the camera, but ends up with the camera behind and then above them as they look down on the Senate floor below, the camera turning and sweeping across the room from left to right. This technique makes use of camera movement within a single shot to accomplish what would more usually be done by the use of shot/reverse shot patterns, and the camera's freedom of movement within a space which appears to extend in all directions is simultaneously powerful and self-effacing, the plenitude of the narrative world at our disposal seeming to reduce the camera to a roving viewpoint within it, rather than an anchored production space with a blind space behind it. Thus Preminger's 180-degree turns within the spaces of the narrative world, as well as the many movements of characters along the axis between background and foreground, give a vivid sense of space extending in all directions around the camera, obliterating its own place entirely except as a mobile viewpoint which we are invited to share. Whether this sense of our having free access to the film's world – a kind of privileged objectivity – is more apparent than real will need to be examined more carefully.

The next cut to ground level, as Munson enters the Senate through a door at the rear, uses a low angle to include a clock and motto above and behind him, with the faces of Dolly and her friends to the left of the clock, the camera then levelling out to exclude the gallery as Munson talks with Strickland and some other men. Back in the gallery, the women's talk reflects the camera's interest in space. When the seating arrangements for each political party on the right and left of the aisle respectively are pointed out to Madame Barré (Michele Montau), the wife of the newly appointed French ambassador, she asks in surprise, 'Does America have so many leftists?' Lady Maudulayne (Hilary Eaves) is quick to reply, 'Oh, no, darling, it's purely geographical. I mean they're all Republicans or Democrats – no Communists or anything of that sort.' The explanations which Dolly and Lady Maudulayne offer as the scene proceeds and the Vice-President takes up the chair downstairs are partly for our benefit, not simply for the French ambassador's wife, yet the issue of whether Leffingwell is indeed a Communist – or, at least, had Communist tendencies in the past – will be central to the subcommittee's investigations. Although our privileged

FIGURE 14 *Brig Anderson on the far right of the frame, and the Senator from Hawaii on the far left*

knowledge of the truth will quickly outpace that of the majority of Senators on the floor, at every stage our knowledge will be more partial than we
realise at the time.

The question of inclusion and exclusion broached by Lady Maudulayne's
remark is also implicit in the women's relegation to the gallery upstairs,
the Senate turning out, unsurprisingly, to be an almost exclusively white
male affair, although one woman Senator appears later. The racial otherness of a single Hispanic Senator and that of Senator Kanaho (Tiki Santos)
from Hawaii are also evident, although clearly exceptional. The presence of
Kanaho is of particular interest, and he alone is signalled as 'other' by both
his physical appearance and his accent. Our first view of him occurs right
after the moment discussed earlier, in which Tom August and Bob Munson
ask Brig Anderson to chair the subcommittee and the ceiling is included
in the shot. As they re-enter the Senate, we follow Munson to his seat as
Senator Orrin Knox (Edward Andrews) is speaking and, when Munson rises
to his feet to ask for permission to speak and Knox replies, both Anderson
and Kanaho are included in the frame, their inclusion together repeated at
several points in the later meetings of the subcommittee itself. So, while
Leffingwell's secret past is being uncovered and investigated, Anderson's

homosexual encounter years before, when he was in the army and sta-
tioned in Hawaii, is obliquely inscribed in the film, at the level of the image,
by the suggestiveness of his juxtaposition with the Senator from Hawaii in
the frame, a juxtaposition which is meaningless in terms of the workings
of the plot and unreadable at any level on our first viewing of the film. Retrospectively, however, the image resonates with significance, not least the
association of Anderson's sexuality with notions of otherness in relation to
the straight white male world of the Senate.

The Senate scenes intermingle public performances and private com-
mentaries upon them, as we overhear the casual asides and more sustained conversations of Senators reacting to speeches being made elsewhere in the frame or offscreen. There is much to hold our attention in the
multiple planes of action and reaction laid out before us, with numerous
key characters simultaneously visible at various distances from the camera.
The entrances and exits of some characters motivate corresponding camera
movements (for example, Munson's arrival and walk to his seat), while
others are left unmarked as background details to be noticed or not (for
instance, the arrival of the Senator from Hawaii in the course of Orrin Knox's
speech). The atmosphere in these early Senate scenes is generally good-
humoured, with Anderson joining in the laughter as Lafe Smith speaks
of Seab's 'aged crust of prejudice', although the camera draws back from
Seab himself as he refers to Leffingwell as an evil man. From the applause
which greets Seab's call for Leffingwell's rejection, we dissolve to Dolly and
others at her party that night.

Although many of the same people whom we see in the various Senate
scenes are amongst Dolly's guests, the Senate's virtual segregation of men
and women is now repaired by their interminglings at Dolly's party, and the
camera's movements as Dolly walks through the crowd are initially more
purposefully motivated by her actions alone. The sense of Dolly presiding
over her own domain is reinforced by the way she silences an over-argu-
mentative Van Ackerman with a parody of political rhetoric – 'Would the
Senator yield the floor?' – while Van Ackerman's empty posturing is under-
lined by his clutching an unlit pipe by the bowl (which he does in other
scenes as well), the pipe an unconvincing and self-consciously adopted

emblem of his supposed authority, in contrast to the purely utilitarian cigarette which Munson smokes elsewhere in the film. However, Dolly's con-
fident orchestrations of the party and her glittering guests merely emphasises how powerless she is in other contexts: her party and the male world
of 'party politics' have little in common besides the partially overlapping
personnel.

When Munson returns to the darkened house later that night, and we
are suddenly made aware of his relationship with Dolly, her refusal to marry
him and disrupt their backstairs romance may also reveal a resistance on
her part to what seems like a demotion to the role of politician's wife. The
ignominy of this role is most incisively etched in the impossible position of
Brig Anderson's wife Ellen, who tells Brig at one point: 'What do you think I
live for? You're my whole life, you and Pidge, there isn't anything else.' It is
consistent with the film's interest in spatial correlatives to the relationships
amongst its characters that the corollary of her desperate self-effacement
takes the form of a spatial metaphor: 'All I want to do is to stand beside
you, and you give me no place to stand'. The visual parallels between Munson's arrival at Dolly's silent and shadowy house and Brig's arrival home
after he stands up to the President's demand that Leffingwell be approved
are striking, and we will need to explore this further when we come to the
later scene. Indeed, the relationship between Dolly and Munson is oddly
disconnected from the rest of the film and is never followed up in any way,
its sole purpose seeming to be as preparation and context for the scene
with Ellen and Brig.

There are several other pointers to Brig Anderson's centrality to the
film's dramatic and thematic structures which prepare us for the later revelations, not least Van Ackerman's surprisingly blatant threats – for example, his remarks to Munson: 'Any time old Brig isn't co-operating, I might
be able to change his mind,' and 'If you want Brig whipped into line, I've
got the whip on file'. To this must be added the President's inadvertently
ironic comment to Anderson: 'Well, maybe there's nothing in your young
life you'd like to conceal. We're not all of us that fortunate,' the President
himself hiding the seriousness of his illness from the Vice-President and
others. All of these remarks precede our knowledge that Anderson has

anything to hide, which only becomes impossible to miss when he arrives home after the meeting with the President and Ellen tells him about a strange phone call she had that day, a bit of information forcefully supported by the film's visual rhetoric at that point, as we will see. So it is easy to take Van Ackerman's threats as empty bluster (part of a false front he presents, like his unlit pipe).

Similarly, the irony of the President's remark, like so much else in the film, is only apparent in retrospect, and his comment initially comes across as a more generalised warning against the self-righteousness which Anderson seems to be displaying at this point. Thus, Anderson is unyielding when he insists that Leffingwell 'lied under oath,' although the President replies by asking him to consider why he lied: 'You think he should let himself be ruined just because he flirted with Communism a long time ago?' Munson later willingly admits his own moral inconsistency in standing by the President by explaining to Anderson: 'I love the man. I guess I can stretch my responsibility a little. Enough to help him,' while Anderson replies, 'I'm sorry, but mine won't stretch.' Nevertheless, although his lack of flexibility – which worryingly links him to Van Ackerman's dogmatic rigidity – reveals a degree of over-confidence in his own moral correctness, it is only to his wife that he expresses anything precisely like pride and, when he half-jokingly boasts of having defied the President, his behaviour comes across as a boyishly vulnerable attempt to impress her with his importance which is easy to forgive. In fact, it can more readily be understood, in retrospect, as evidence both of his uncertainty about being a husband worthy of her love and respect and, less overtly, of the homosexual relationship in his past which he does so much to suppress, these inner conflicts making him a sympathetic character in ways that Van Ackerman can never be.

The fact that Anderson's intolerance is of his own homosexuality as much as of anything else makes him both victim and perpetrator of his own oppression, and his desire to remain morally 'pure' in opposing Leffingwell's appointment may be seen as part of a deeper process of disavowal, a desire to unmake the past while withholding this chance from Leffingwell. Thus, it may be fruitful to see him as projecting onto Leffingwell the sense he harbours within himself of his own impurity and unworthiness, with

Leffingwell's punishment offering him the possibility of being cleansed of his own 'sin' while simultaneously allowing himself to feel he has done the right thing. Indeed, one of the questions he asks Leffingwell at his hearing before the subcommittee – 'Do you think we should discontinue pride in our freedoms and our way of life?' – can easily be related to his own situation and the jokey display of pride he will later offer to his wife. All of this will be examined in detail, but first the intervening scenes between Munson's late-night arrival at Dolly's darkened house and Anderson's arrival home need some attention, as they are centrally concerned with Leffingwell's secret past, the focus of both the Senators' deliberations and the plot.

From Dolly's house, as she and Munson embrace, the film dissolves to a scene of bustle and anticipation, as the subcommittee chaired by Brig Anderson prepares to convene. Rather than going through the sequence in exhaustive detail, it is sufficient to suggest a few aspects of Preminger's treatment which seem especially significant. In the earlier presentation of the Senate, the rows of Senators and spectators were all facing forward towards the Vice-President's desk in a series of separate planes orientated in the direction of a single focal point. The members of the subcommittee, in contrast, are seated along one side of a long rectangular table which is directly opposite the witness table, the participants at each table looking across at one another and backed by press, spectators, and secretaries, with television cameras and flash-guns visible in a number of shots. Seab Cooley, in particular, although not an official member of the subcommittee, is presented as something of a media star, with press photographers gathered behind him at the far end of the main table at right angles to the side where Anderson presides on the left, the flash cameras surrounding Seab like a frame. Depending on which table the camera faces head-on, the other table and those seated there are excluded from the shot, although oblique-angle shots are sometimes used to include Seab as a background presence at the far end when some of the members of the subcommittee speak.

Thus, extensive cross-cutting between characters tends to be used rather more than was the case in the scenes on the Senate floor, where major characters were more frequently located within the multiple planes of a single shot. Further, there are fewer arrivals and departures in the course of the subcommittee debate, so both camera and character movements, when they do occur, tend to stand out much more from the generally static physical set-up. Whereas the scenes on the Senate floor involved an exploratory camera and an intricate interplay of actions and reactions, performances and asides, the subcommittee scenes appear more starkly confrontational, with the question-and-answer format reflected in the pattern of cuts between speakers in separate compartments of space. Nevertheless, a sense of three-dimensional space and complexity of point of view is maintained through the continuity of some of the characters' speeches across the cuts, as well as by the variety of ways in which participants, witnesses and spectators are spatially orientated within the Senate subcommittee chamber.

Although witnesses approach and leave the table as they are called and dismissed, the only prominent Senators to stand or move around in the course of the proceedings are Fred Van Ackerman and Seab Cooley, the former in anger and the latter as part of a self-consciously dramatic performance whose effects are carefully calculated. Seab is a small background figure in some of the shots that include Anderson and his colleagues on the left side of the frame but, at other times, Seab begins to speak as an offscreen voice intruding on spaces from which he is physically absent, a transcendence over space which appears to give him considerable power and dramatic effectiveness. Although Seab has no control over whether he is included in or excluded from the frame, he is able to indulge his flair for the dramatic in other ways, most fulsomely when the subcommittee have reconvened after lunch and Leffingwell seems on the point of receiving the subcommittee's blessing.

Leffingwell had earlier reacted with what seemed like genuine bemusement to the revelation that a man named Herbert Gelman had sent a telegram to one of the Senators claiming that Leffingwell was a Communist at the University of Chicago many years before and, since Gelman had proved impossible to trace, he was dismissed by Leffingwell as a crank. Now, however, just as Seab has said he has no further questions and the subcommittee are on the point of adjournment, Seab pulls his rabbit out of the hat: although he said he had no more questions, he has one more witness to call, naming him as Herbert Gelman (Burgess Meredith) and thus revealing himself as the force behind the mysterious telegram to his colleague, who reacts with anger at having been unwittingly used. Throughout the initial questioning of Gelman, in contrast to the use of more anonymous characters in the background throughout the rest of the sequence, Leffingwell is visible to the right of the frame behind him. However, rather than this providing us with simultaneous access to Gelman's testimony and Leffingwell's reactions, the strategy merely emphasises Leffingwell's unreadability at this stage in the film, and we remain uncertain whether Gelman or Leffingwell has been telling the truth.

Seab's outrageous showmanship could not present more of a contrast with Leffingwell's calm reasonableness as he asks for an hour to prepare his response to Gelman's accusations. Yet the irony which, once again, we are only aware of in retrospect, is that Gelman's accusations are largely true and Leffingwell is fully aware of his own guilt. So the differences between Seab and Leffingwell are differences of performance style – one performs showmanship, while the other performs sincerity – rather than that Seab is lying whereas Leffingwell is telling the truth, and Seab is clearly displeased when Leffingwell's performance receives even more applause than his own. That Leffingwell is performing just as much as Seab, and even more convincingly, becomes quickly evident to us when he visits Hardiman Fletcher (Paul McGrath) – one of the other members of the Communist cell in Chicago – during the hour he has been given to prepare his response, and he tells him of his intention to tell the subcommittee the truth.

Although Fletcher greets Leffingwell warmly, in the opening long take, the scene quickly reverts to the confrontational cross-cutting already evident at the subcommittee meeting and ends chillingly when, after Fletcher has pointed out that Gelman's testimony, although essentially true, was shot through with inconsistencies and minor lies, he gives his advice: 'Destroy him. It's easy for you, Leff.' Although he justifies his hard-hearted position by explaining that he has a family to feed, the glimpse we get of his children when they ask him to settle an argument between them at the beginning of the scene suggests domestic disharmony and lack of communication, and Fletcher's response – 'Now, if you kids don't go in there and behave, I'm gonna tell mother' – aligns him with Van Ackerman, Seab and the President himself as they attempt to get what they want through bullying and threats.

Once Leffingwell has destroyed Gelman's credibility on the stand, the action moves predominantly backstage in a series of manoeuvrings; some of them are explicitly shown, while others are merely implied after the fact. For example, Leffingwell tells the President he has lied, Seab discovers Fletcher's identity and pressures him to ring up Brig Anderson and confess, Anderson postpones the subcommittee vote as a result and tells the President that Leffingwell's nomination will have to be withdrawn, and the President sends Fletcher out of the country so that he will not be available as a witness against Leffingwell. As Leffingwell's past becomes more and more of an open secret, with Seab, Anderson, Munson and the President all in on the truth, Leffingwell becomes more and more peripheral to the film.

Just as Munson's relationship with Dolly Harrison oddly fizzles out as a narrative concern, functioning mainly to provide a context for Anderson's relationship with his wife, so too does Leffingwell's past. Its emergence through Gelman provides a preparation for the emergence of Anderson's secret in the form of Ray, his homosexual lover from the past who has been 'bought' by Van Ackerman. Van Ackerman, who acts in ignorance of the details of the subcommittee deadlock, is the instrument of Anderson's undoing yet, equally, he is Preminger's tool in the undoing of the narrative itself – at least in terms of the trajectory it seemed to be following so far – as its concentration on Leffingwell is increasingly derailed, and Leffingwell will only appear in one more scene.

The scene where Brig Anderson returns home at night after the confrontation with the President begins with the familiar interplay of left-right movements and those along the axis into the depth of the frame, as his car approaches the camera and then turns right and slightly away from the camera into the driveway of his home. As he moves towards the house with an eager loping stride and a smile on his face, he presents an image of self-satisfaction and youthful enthusiasm at the prospect of sharing his recent triumph with his wife. However, as soon as we cut to the darkened interior of the house, as Brig enters and locks the door behind him, we are distanced from his mood of cheerful anticipation with a sense of foreboding, while the door and adjacent panel, comprised largely of panes of glass, seem worryingly flimsy and inadequate to the job of keeping his family safe. The shadowy lighting is even more apparent as he opens his daughter's door and we see him from our position inside, Brig appearing as a silhouette in the doorway. After bending over Pidge to tuck her in, Brig stands and is engulfed by the darkness in the upper half of the room. The sentimental music is at odds with the visual presentation of his body merging with the darkness, and he leaves the room as he entered it, as a silhouette.

From this ominous beginning, we cut to the master bedroom, as Brig opens the door and enters, edging in sideways with his back to his wife so as not to wake her up in her single bed on the far side of the room. Above his own single bed by the door is an odd picture of an upside-down flower hanging from its stem. As he moves towards the bathroom in the background of the shot, to the left of Ellen's bed, she turns on the light. A very abrupt cut as he re-enters the bedroom and leans down to kiss her reinforces the sense of something being not quite right, and Brig walks to the window, his tie loosened and his shirt unbuttoned, as he smiles and begins to brag about his stand-off with the President. Despite his boyish pride, his back is turned to Ellen as he speaks, producing an awkwardness which seems in contradiction with the playful swagger of his words. As Brig takes off his shirt and walks back to the bathroom, his shadow visible on the wall to his left, Ellen follows him in: 'I had a very strange phone call, Brig.' From this we cut to the most resonant image in the sequence – a shot of Brig looking at himself in the bathroom mirror – which continues throughout the rest of the scene, a scene which seems to constitute the thematic heart of the film.

The use of the mirror is particularly marked since there is no sustained thematic use of a mirror anywhere else in the film, despite the emphasis throughout on other elements of setting and decor, with doors and corridors being especially salient and suggestive. Here, the composition is

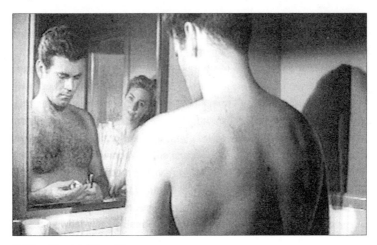

FIGURE 15 *Mirror shot of Brig and Ellen*

meticulously contrived so that, while Ellen's reflection is visible for most of the shot in a small corner of the mirror, she remains otherwise offscreen. The foreground is dominated by Brig's broad naked back, with his shadow on the wall to the right behind him, and his nakedness is doubly empha- sised by our view of his chest in the mirror as well. The sexualising of Brig through the display of his body is not matched by an equivalent sexualis- ing of Ellen. Her hair is pulled back in a girlish ponytail and, as she follows him to the bathroom, the camera's unkind view of her from behind endows her with a plumpness around the hips where her unflattering nightgown is pulled in at the waist.

The combination of these hints of sexual immaturity and yet potential dowdiness reinforce a sense of their marriage as sexually disappointing for them both, and this impression is confirmed in a conversation they have later in the film when Ellen suspects Brig of having betrayed her with another woman, acknowledging: 'I know we haven't had an exciting mar- riage'. Her voice, too, in the present scene, has an almost petulant quality, a clingy plaintiveness, and the fact that Ellen has gone to bed while at the same time lying awake in the darkness waiting for Brig to come home sug- gests a certain deviousness of purpose, as if she wants to present a façade of normality – yet a normality of separate beds and independent routines with little reason to stay awake for his late-night returns – while knowing that something is very wrong between them and remaining vigilant.

When we first see them together in the mirror, his smile is gone and the eyes of both of them are lowered. For the rest of the scene, Brig looks at her only as a reflection in the mirror as they talk, rather than at Ellen herself offscreen. The many details of his uneasy body language – the visible tightening of his jaw, the nervous laugh, the exaggerated vigour with which he brushes his teeth – make it absolutely clear that, for all his self-righteousness over Leffingwell's lies at the hearing, Brig is himself telling lies to his wife. The whole scene appears over-determined and increasingly burdened with an accumulation of signs and signifiers of the bleakness and lack of passion in their married life. At the same time, the presentation of Brig's body as a passive sexual object to be looked at – and the narcissistic use of the mirror which, by doubling him, allows us an image of Brig face-to-face with his own naked body – is rich in insinuations about the nature of what happened in Hawaii. So the scene tells us everything there is to know, but in a guarded and implicit fashion, displacing meanings into bodily postures and aspects of the composition and decor which are crucial to the emotional texture of the scene while difficult to pin down with any certainty. The atmosphere is highly charged, while the conversation is inhibited and characterised by prevarication and constraint.

All of this looks very different from the earlier scene of Bob Munson coming home to Dolly Harrison, despite the superficial similarities between them – the men in both scenes returning to a darkened house where the women are waiting up for them in their night clothes – which seem to be offering themselves to us in order to be compared. What Munson finds at the heart of Dolly's house is a cosy and welcoming haven set against the vast shadowy coldness of the rest of the house, where Dolly entertains so well upon the public stage and which we presume to be a legacy from her late husband. Dolly herself is relaxed and attractive, and the physicality of the relationship is quickly evident, both in Dolly's remark that he is 'as virile as a billy-goat' and in the affectionate warmth with which they embrace as she sits on his lap on the comfortable couch. Their honesty and good humour persist even as she remains adamant in her refusal to marry him, and both the deep gravelly resonance of Walter Pidgeon's voice and the low rich tones of Gene Tierney's reinforce our sense of the maturity and robustness of their middle-aged romance and their suitability to one another.

It is a moving and pleasurable scene, with none of the alienation and fragility so obvious in the relationship of Ellen and Brig, and its preconditions seem to be precisely that Dolly has her independence and a life of her own, and that their relationship is a thing apart, unembedded in marriage and Washington society, so that there are no burdensome conventional expectations from outside for the couple to live up to. Where much of the film offers us views of characters located within large and complexly intersecting spaces much bigger than themselves, suggesting that they are pawns of political institutions over which they have little control, Munson and Dolly do appear to have carved out a private space which is safe from such intrusive outside management.

In contrast, what Brig finds at the heart of his house is a bedroom as cold and shadowy as anywhere else. The fact that the key scene in front of the mirror takes place in the adjoining bathroom makes its atmosphere appear even more clinical and repressive. The sight of Brig looking at himself in the mirror is thus significantly different from the two equivalent shots from *My Darling Clementine* which we looked at in Chapter 1. There we saw how Wyatt Earp's reflection integrated him into his surroundings through an image of wholeness and reconciliation, whereas Doc Holliday confronted the darkness within himself and the distance he had travelled from the promises of his past to his present illness and isolation. Brig's mirror image, like Doc's, has a mocking quality, but Brig himself stops short of confronting it, adopting a sort of wilful blindness to his past, so that his reflection in the mirror takes on an opaque and defensive aspect, Brig blocking out thought and will as he brushes his teeth like a rigid mechanical doll. This effect of Brig appearing to block out the past is repeated when Van Ackerman's stooge telephones him in the Senate cafeteria in a later scene, and tells him that they have the 'stuff' from Hawaii and will use it if they have to. Brig's response – 'Use what? What? I ... I don't know what ...' – presents us with such a convincing air of puzzlement on his part that it is hard to know whether Brig is merely giving a good performance of sincerity, like Leffingwell before him, or whether he genuinely believes his own denials.

What has been described earlier as the heart of the film takes us to the heart of Brig's house and, indeed, to the heart of his marriage. What we have found is a secret desire which threatens to reduce the up-and-coming young white male so full of confidence at the start of the scene to a figure of otherness and marginality, similar to his wife – whose identity is so terrifyingly empty and peripheral to the film's centres of power and influence that it has virtually disappeared ('You're my whole life ... there isn't anything else ... you give me no place to stand,' and so on). Brig is hovering on the edge of a similar existential abyss which he is desperately trying not to acknowledge as he too, increasingly, comes to feel he has no place to stand. Ironically, it is likely that the exposure of his homosexual relationship in the past would cause no more than a momentary ripple of gossip in the present. Munson's curt rebuke to Van Ackerman – 'We could introduce a resolution to censure and expel you, but we don't want Brig Anderson's tired old sin made public, whatever it was' – certainly implies that compassion would outweigh condemnation, at least on the part of the Senate's more liberal and humane representatives.

Throughout the film, public and private spaces are intimately linked, not only through the intrusiveness of the world of politics into the home life of many of the characters, but also through the camera's strategy of pausing in the course of its wanderings through public spaces – most specifically, the Senate – to discover private conversations and groupings within them. The scene in the Senate cafeteria in which Brig Anderson is telephoned and threatened by one of Van Ackerman's men is a good example of this and has many additional features already identified elsewhere (for example, the sense of a strong and significant background presence in the shot). The scene occurs at a point when Anderson has been trying courageously, and with increasing desperation, to maintain his integrity by refusing to allow the vote on Leffingwell, in the hope that his stated intention to call Fletcher as a witness against Leffingwell will cause the President to withdraw the nomination before Anderson's blackmailer has a chance to act on his threats. However, Seab Cooley disabuses him of this by revealing that Fletcher has been sent abroad, and Anderson's earlier boyish pride at having the President on the run is exposed as having been naïvely founded upon false hopes and an underestimation of the President's cunning.

From the scene with Seab we dissolve to Anderson quickly walking down a corridor towards the camera, then to screen right into the cafeteria, where he accosts Munson and accuses him of complicity in sending Fletcher away. We then cut to Van Ackerman and his cronies at a table in an adjoining room, one of them getting up and walking towards the camera, then to screen left past Munson and Anderson as Munson insists he knows nothing about Fletcher's departure. This is followed by a cut to Lafe Smith and Danta at yet another table as the telephone rings, Lafe rising to answer it and pass it over to Brig, while Van Ackerman's group is visible in the background watching. In the same take, Anderson walks to the phone, his shadow on the wall, and the camera moves in closer to him so that the inclusion of Van Ackerman and his pals, which was previously a less obtrusive part of the background, becomes impossible to miss, as they are clearly seen studying Anderson behind his back. We then cut to Van Ackerman's man whistling a tune as he leaves the phone booth and walks past Anderson to Van Ackerman's table, while Anderson returns to Munson, insisting he will not be scared off, as Munson looks puzzled and taken aback.

The complexity of the scene in terms of the movements of camera and characters provides an underpinning and reinforcement of the complex intertwining of its various narrative strands. The clarity with which the film manages to present such a large number of memorable and sharply differentiated characters with such a variety of motivations and political agendas is remarkable and shows considerable respect for the intelligence and alertness of its audience. It was suggested earlier that Leffingwell's story – the story of whether his nomination for Secretary of State will be spoiled by his flirtation with Communism in the past – is increasingly displaced by Anderson's, which centres on how his naïve and over-confident sense of his own integrity is put to the test by his fear of public exposure of what he considers to be a deeply shameful and humiliating secret. Nevertheless, the two stories (Leffingwell's and Anderson's) are both part of another, larger one, that of the homogeneity of the Senate and the way it deals with deviance from its rules. The rules of inclusion and exclusion from the august spaces of the Senate involve other characters as well, including women like Dolly Harrison who are relegated to the gallery upstairs, and the token Senators whose anomalous race or gender shows them to be exceptions that prove the rule.

Anderson's trip to New York City to find Ray Shaff (John Granger), the man from his past, is the point when these issues come to a head. The gay club where Anderson tracks him down is a kind of antithetical counterpart to the (virtually) all-male Senate, representing as it does a world of marginality and transgression, rather than a centre of power and law. As he enters the club he approaches the camera along a corridor and, in a move reminiscent of the one which accompanied our first view of the Senate floor when Dolly and her friends looked down on it from the gallery above, the camera turns so that it ends up half behind Brig as the club opens up before him slightly below and on the right of the frame. Thus, the prospect of his immersion in this alternative world momentarily places him in the position of Dolly and the other women excluded from the institutional power of the straight white men in the Senate, a relegation to the sidelines of government and society which would threaten his already precarious self esteem.

Throughout the shot, Frank Sinatra's voice is heard singing: 'Let me hear a voice, a secret voice, a voice that will say come to me and be what I need you to be'. The lazy musical cadences, overlaid with dissonance, and the ambiguous lyrics can be taken as a mocking example of the sudden mutability of Brig Anderson's world, with order and stability dissolving into chaos, while what Sinatra presumably intended as a heterosexual love song appears to slide into an expression of homosexual desire. Anderson flees in horror from this vision of what he has it within himself to become, his horror disproportionate to the actual presentation of the club. When Ray follows him out, Anderson flings him aside, refusing to listen to Ray's reasons for agreeing to be part of Van Ackerman's scheme: 'I needed money, Brig. Well, you wouldn't see me. I kept calling ...'. So Ray is not just Brig's exploiter, but his victim as well, a spurned lover to whom the film extends some sympathy.

In the matter of Leffingwell's destructive cross-examination of Gelman, both the honourable politician with good intentions and the broken man whose credibility he is forced to destroy were figures of sympathy and now, once again, the film refuses to divide its characters into antagonistic categories of right and wrong. Gelman's surprise when he found out that Leffingwell had got him his job at the Treasury Department, after he was let go from his previous job at Leffingwell's instigation, made clear that his motive had been to get back at the man who fired him, and that he now feels some regret. This is not so far away from Ray's stated motive in colluding in the blackmail of Brig, as both Gelman and Ray react to their rejections at the hands of other men.

Our passage through the film's network of branching narratives and spaces is abruptly blocked when Anderson kills himself in his office on his return from New York, his death presented as an offscreen event which is signalled to us by the sight of the security guard pounding on the locked bathroom door in Anderson's office suite. The numerous examples of movements through doors elsewhere in the film – the sense of intricate connected spaces and the camera's freedom within them – make the locked door a particularly striking marker of finality, of a definitive end to Anderson's story, at least from his point of view. That the suicide takes place in a bathroom is also striking, reminding us of the mirror scene in Brig's bathroom at home when the past finally caught up with him, despite his dogged refusal to acknowledge it at the time.

The film's final scene is when the Senate votes on whether to *advise and consent* to the subcommittee recommendation that Leffingwell's nomination be approved, and it is inter-cut with shots of the President listening to a live broadcast of the proceedings in his office. In the course of these events, the President dies offscreen, like Anderson, and the Vice-President – now elevated to the presidency – refuses to break the tied vote, preferring to choose his own nominee and, in the process, to become his own man. With Leffingwell out of the running, Anderson and the President dead, and all of Munson's considerable moral authority turned against Van

Ackerman for his shameful role in Anderson's death, a number of stories have been resolved, while another story – the new President's search for a Secretary of State and for a new version of himself – is just beginning.

So the film effectively ends where it began, although some of the characters have left the stage or at any rate changed roles, and the cyclical structure which is suddenly imposed upon the film's narrative locates the characters within a context much larger than themselves and with much less sense of any straightforward narrative progression effectively motivated by their individual concerns. This sense of the narrative being determined from elsewhere is consonant with what was discussed earlier regarding the characters' locations in larger institutional spaces than the pathways measured out by their own steps alone. The film's treatments of space and narrative are thus mutually consistent but, although human agency is seen to be tempered by more powerful institutional and ideological frameworks, the importance of moral responsibility and of such human values as tolerance and compassion remains, with a great deal of weight given to Munson's condemnation of Van Ackerman for putting political expediency first.

Advise and Consent is a remarkable achievement. It is a film of retrospection, openly inviting us to revisit it as a condition of our understanding it fully, with much of its significance withheld or unreadable during an initial viewing. After Seab produces Gelman as his surprise witness at the meeting of the Senate subcommittee, and Munson reacts by calling him an 'old buzzard', Seab replies: 'Us old buzzards can see a mouse dyin' from ten thousand feet up. Us old buzzards have the sharpest eyes in creation. Right now I'm studying the terrain.' There is no camera positioning in the course of the film which gives us a distanced overhead perspective such as he describes, but the final moments of the film as the Senate adjourns and begins to clear out do come close. As Munson moves for an adjournment, following the announcement of the President's death, the camera rises and pulls back, then rises higher to include the gallery as well, before settling down into a still position as the credits roll and men in shirtsleeves clear the desks. The camera's partial approximation of the viewpoint described by Seab in his earlier comments suggests, perhaps, that Preminger is trying

FIGURE 16 *Seab Cooley finds out that Brig is dead.*

to sharpen our eyes as well, while encouraging us – like Seab – to study the terrain. Thus the final shot provides a retrospective gloss on the film as a whole.

We need to take this one step further, since it is no accident that Seab is the one to speak these words. If we consider the moment when Seab first hears of Anderson's death, while playing cards at Dolly Harrison's house, we will notice that his expression is particularly inscrutable as the camera singles him out, his eyes lowered and his brow slightly furrowed as he continues to smoke without giving anything away. We can only speculate at this stage about the extent to which he feels his own behaviour may have contributed to Anderson's death. However, during the crucial Leffingwell vote, he abandons his earlier vindictiveness towards the candidate and apologises for it to the Senate. Munson's appreciative response confirms Seab's words as evidence of his openness to moral persuasion, and of his willingness to rethink his position and take responsibility for the consequences of his actions. Despite his imperfections, Seab becomes a figure who is capable of moral growth and whose sharp eyes and attention to human frailty are put to good purpose in the end. This is the challenge which the film sets its viewers as well.

Suggestions for further reading

In the 1960s the British film journal *Movie* championed Preminger's work, and Robin Wood (1962) offers an early appreciative response to *Advise and Consent*. More recently, however, it is mainly Preminger's work within the genre of film noir which has received critical attention (for example Kaplan (1998) includes some references to *Laura*, and Cameron (1992) has more extended discussions of *Fallen Angel* and *Angel Face*). It is difficult to single out any particular book or article which deals more generally with the construction of a film's spaces through such cinematic means as camerawork, editing, the composition of the image and so on, since this is an important aspect of most close readings. The BFI Film Classics series, for example, provides a range of such accounts, and is as useful a starting point as any. In addition, Wilson (1986) and Pye (2000) offer close readings of specific films as a way of exploring issues around point of view, which is an essential aspect of cinematic constructions of space.

4 THE SPACE OF THE SPECTATOR: DIEGETIC AND NON-DIEGETIC, VIRTUAL AND REAL

The aim of this book so far has been to provide a few ideas about some of the ways Hollywood films create and present significant spaces and how these presentations relate to narrative structures and thematic concerns. Although a degree of generalisation has been possible, we have also seen the importance of close study of particular films in order to appreciate the effects of spatial and narrative decisions when combined with all the idiosyncratic specifics of a given script, soundtrack, set of performances, directorial sensibility, and so on. The sorts of questions which have been raised about settings, dramaturgical schemas and more purely cinematic strategies can be asked about any films, but the fully fleshed out answers we come up with will differ from case to case. Although we have accorded a privileged position to individual films – and therefore to their narrative worlds and modes of representation – a film's narrative world will nec-essarily exceed those portions of it which we see onscreen at any given moment. Thus, in the discussion of *Advise and Consent*, the way in which its camerawork keeps offscreen space alive was examined. It is now necessary to say a bit more about certain potential ambiguities in our understanding of offscreen space.

When we watch a traditional narrative film – a Hollywood film, say, from the so-called classical period – there are two fundamental senses of off-screen space which such a film works at making us forget: the space of the film's production (the studio floor, for example) and the viewing space which we occupy as we watch (the film theatre, say). It would be quite a shock – at least in the context of the sort of films under consideration – to find that as the camera panned across the spaces of the narrative world, bringing previously excluded spaces into view, we suddenly saw cranes, lights, and studio personnel, with the narrative world suddenly exposed as a set or roped-off location. Nevertheless, too fulsome a presentation of the film's narrative world as an unbounded independent space can be equally unsettling. Thus, in the discussion of *Advise and Consent* in Chapter 3, we saw examples of 180-degree turns made by Preminger's camera within the spaces of the narrative world which have an almost uncanny feel to them in their suggestion of a unified three-dimensional space surrounding the camera viewpoint. This explicitly brings to our attention the apparent absence of a production space behind the camera's back. At such moments, we may find ourselves wondering 'How can this be?' at the same time as we give ourselves up to the illusion of the narrative world filling all available space both onscreen and off. Despite the suppression of any explicit acknowledgement of an offscreen production space in most traditional narrative films, we implicitly take it for granted as a given, which is really no more than to say that we never fully forget we are watching a film. Indeed, some comedies playfully undermine the tacit collusion between us and the films we view which, to some extent at least, offer themselves to us as the world and which we agree to take as such (a collusion based upon our mutually knowing that this is not really so, yet agreeing not to 'speak' of it together), and such comic playfulness may take us aback far less than when the illusion that we are watching the world and not a film becomes too convincing.

Our implicit acceptance of the production space behind the camera is partly evidenced by the way we take for granted that the narrative world will generally be orientated in our direction (presenting its 'face' towards the camera, towards us), and it can have a disturbing effect when characters either too pointedly keep their backs to us or approach the camera too closely. We saw an example of the latter in Chapter 2 when Parris Mitchell seemed to be stopped in his tracks as he came too near to the camera at the end of the childhood sequence in *Kings Row*. Although this was discussed as offering a spatial equivalent to Parris's dimly realised feeling of ideological constraint in a world he does not fully comprehend, it is also a moment that makes us uncomfortably aware of his impingement upon our own safe space as spectators.

The cinema or living room where we find ourselves as we watch a film is the second example of an offscreen space whose existence is rarely acknowledged explicitly within such narrative films themselves. A similar tacit agreement prevails, an agreement only occasionally breached, again mainly in comedies, where we may find ourselves from time to time the targets of a character's direct address.

Yet this account is still not fully accurate, since numerous further techniques which are by no means restricted to comedies – not least the use of voice-over narrators – may also function to openly solicit our attention and thereby acknowledge our presence offscreen. Rhetorical close-ups of significant details provide another example of such direct address, in this case by the film or director, rather than a character: there are many more. The question as to whether there are significant differences between our attention being solicited by a character within the narrative world or by the film itself is an important one, and it relates to a distinction which is well established within the academic discipline of film studies: the distinction between diegetic and non-diegetic aspects of films.

Diegetic and non-diegetic

This subject was implicitly touched on in earlier chapters through the distinction made between settings and cinematic space. A film's diegesis is the narrative world and all that happens within it – those aspects of a film which, at least in principle, are accessible to the characters – while the non-diegetic is all that falls outside it and is aimed exclusively at the viewer. Susan Hayward describes the diegesis as 'narration, the content of the narrative, the fictional world as described inside the story. In film it refers to all that is really going on on-screen, that is, to fictional reality' (1996: 67). Richard Maltby and Ian Craven put the distinction as follows: 'Film criticism uses the terms diegetic and non-diegetic to distinguish between what is included within the imaginary world of the story, whether it is visible onscreen or not, and what is outside it. The terms are often used to identify the source of sounds' (1995: 486).

So the sounds of a piano being played by a character onscreen – but also of a piano heard by an onscreen character but played by someone else in the offscreen portion of the narrative world – are diegetic, while a moody soundtrack which has no source within the narrative world is non-diegetic. So far so good. But what about the music which accompanies the 'Trolley Song' in *Meet Me in St Louis*, say, which could at first be mistaken for non-diegetic soundtrack music as the trolley sets off, but which is quickly accompanied by the passengers singing together, although the orchestral music has no diegetic source either onscreen or off? Warren Buckland (1998: 19) makes a further distinction which may be of help:

> We need to distinguish external diegetic sound from internal diegetic sound. External diegetic sound has a physical origin in the story world ... By contrast, internal diegetic sound has its origin inside a character's mind. In other words, internal diegetic sound refers to subjective sounds – either the rendition of a character's thoughts or imagined sounds. These sounds are still diegetic because they derive from the story world, but they are internal because they cannot be heard by other characters.

However, while this might account for the musical accompaniment to a solo number, there is no reason to suppose that the music in the 'Trolley Song' is likely to be subjectively imagined by any one character more than by any other. As Heather Laing puts it, 'bringing the non-diegetic track into the service of the diegetic song makes the character's relationship to that track ambiguous, calling into question not only the real source of the entire body of music, but also who it is intended to be heard by' (2000: 8).

Are we to take this music as internal diegetic sound heard by all the characters at precisely the same time, since they all begin to sing together? Or, rather, as non-diegetic sound heard only by us so that, although the characters sing in tune with it and at the same pace, they hear only one another's voices, with the happy coincidence of singing and instrumental music being due to Minnelli's intervention for the sake of his audience alone? Neither of these alternatives completely makes sense. It might be objected that what is involved is simply a convention of the genre which allows characters to get on with the musical numbers, and that we are not meant to enquire too closely into its narrative logic. Indeed, Royal S. Brown maintains that the distinction between diegetic and non-diegetic music 'has little meaning in the film musical' (1994: 67). Yet it is precisely this bracketing out of the numbers which is of interest: it is as if the characters are temporarily lifted out of the diegetic world and relocated in another space whose logic obeys a mixture of diegetic and non-diegetic rules.

It seems that there are numerous examples one could cite in the face of which a clear-cut distinction between the diegetic and the non-diegetic breaks down. Victor Perkins uses the phrase '"How" is "What"' as the title to Chapter 6 in *Film as Film* (1972) in order to challenge the duality of content and form. Although this is not quite the same thing as the diegetic versus non-diegetic paradigm which is being called into question, there is considerable congruence between the two dualisms and their shared difficulties in clearly differentiating characters and narrative events from the ways in which they are presented to viewers outside the film. The ambiguities around how to take the music which accompanies characters' songs when it is not played within the physical spaces of the narrative world have their counterparts in the case of a film's representations of characters, places and events which are lifted from their diegetic locations in space and time and relocated elsewhere. Thus flashbacks, like unmotivated music, also seem to hover between diegetic and non-diegetic domains.

Consider the flashbacks in Max Ophuls' *Letter From an Unknown Woman* (1948) which constitute most of the film: are they to be taken as internal diegetic memories experienced by Lisa (Joan Fontaine) when she wrote the letter in the past (for she is dead by the time the film begins)? Or as present internal diegetic memories or imaginings belonging to Stefan (Louis Jourdan) as he reads the letter? Or perhaps as past external diegetic events represented for our benefit and inaccessible to Stefan as he reads about them in the present? Although the events in flashbacks, as a rule, seem meant to be taken as having really happened within the narrative world, their later presentation as flashbacks seems either to internalise them as psychological events, since at the point at which they are evoked they are no longer part of the film's physical reality, or to transform them into non-diegetic events, much as a narrator's voice-over description of events within the diegesis is itself occurring outside of the narrative world – at least if it is addressed to us – even when the narrator is a character from within it. In our current example, because many of the things that happen in the flashbacks cannot have been known by either Stefan or Lisa, it is not possible to see them as internal diegetic events alone.

As Stefan continues to read the letter while the visual images of the past are overlaid upon – and hide – his present activity of reading, the images are more an illustration for us than a direct evocation for him, since to presume he is absorbed in the past thoroughly enough to notice all the detail with which the flashbacks represent it would be to presuppose a state of reverie on his part incompatible with the ongoing linear process of reading, for the flashbacks far surpass what a written account could describe and what the process of reading would leave him time to imaginatively notice and digest. In other words, when reading gives rise to memories of this sort, it disrupts or delays the reading, producing a sort of nostalgic meandering through the imagined world which would seem to make an uninterrupted reading impossible.

It is plausible that there are long pauses of this sort in Stefan's reading, although the intermittent views we have of him whenever we return to him in the present are of a man so engrossed in his reading that it is hard to imagine his attention wandering for as long as would be required. So, while the events in the flashbacks seem incontrovertibly to be external diegetic ones, their status when represented out of sequence – as flashbacks – would appear to be illustrative and non-diegetic, functioning as a sort of quotation of the past, rather than a straightforward presentation, in some sense, of the past itself. In any case, enough has been said to establish the difficulties of being certain either way. As with the music in Minnelli's version of the 'Trolley Song', it is the ontological ambiguity of the flashbacks which is of interest, rather than its resolution one way or the other. Indeed, Perkins (2000: 41) suggests in a discussion of Ophuls' film that:

> It is vital to its effect that it should not solicit a literal reading of its devices, and that it should arrive at a persuasive form while blocking any coherent understanding of the relations between the words of the letter, the speaking voice and the movie's images.

Similarly, it is certainly pertinent that Stanley Cavell should argue that, when Stefan finishes his reading of the letter, he is 'assaulted by a sequence of images from earlier moments in the film' (1996: 81). Although Cavell is not discussing the flashbacks which constitute the main bulk of the film, but rather a quick montage of significant moments very much presenting themselves to Stefan in the present, it is still of interest that what he sees as the focus of Stefan's subjective experience should be described by Cavell as bits of film, rather than bits of the narrative past, so that even this relatively clear example of internal diegetic experience is intermingled with non-diegetic qualities (as if Ophuls were lobbing images at Stefan).

Consideration of flashbacks is further complicated when – as in Alfred Hitchcock's *Stage Fright* (1950) – a flashback is a false representation of the past. Clearly such events cannot be taken as external diegetic, since they never happened within the narrative world (but only on the film set). However, as a deliberate fabrication on the part of Jonathan (Richard Todd), intended to deceive the gullible Eve (Jane Wyman), they are not his internal memory or fantasy either. That is, it is not obvious that he is visualising them (or somehow holding them in his mind) as we are compelled to do, while he speaks. Is this Eve's internal fantasy, based on Jonathan's words, in which case the accuracy of its details is astounding? Or is it Hitchcock's non-diegetic offering to the film's viewers, a visual equivalent to a non-diegetic narrator or piece of music on the soundtrack intended to condition and manipulate our response, as Jonathan's words manipulate Eve's?

Another troubling set of examples, although less common than flashbacks, involves a camera strategy which also undermines our sense of a straightforward separation between what 'really' happens in a film and what lies outside its diegetic world. In John Sayles' *Lone Star* (1996), where at several points both past and present are linked in a single shot, there is an interesting sequence where the camera starts off on an elderly man named Hollis (Clifton James) who is seated at a restaurant table with some friends. As he talks about Charlie Wade (Kris Kristofferson), who was sheriff in the town many years ago, the camera moves to a basket of tortillas on the table while Hollis withdraws his hands from the frame on the left, and Wade's hand reaches towards the basket from the other side of the table (to remove some money hidden amongst the tortillas as Hollis describes Wade's susceptibility to bribes), with a younger version of Hollis just out of shot and revealed through a cut as the scene proceeds. Although all the onscreen events – both past and present – are diegetic, their apparent co-presence goes against the film's diegetic logic (this is not, after all, a science fiction film about time-travel). It is as if a larger imaginary space – a cinematic space – is being evoked which past and present can somehow momentarily cohabit, a bit like the way flashbacks call up past moments and reposition them within an ongoing diegetical present. In the example from *Lone Star*, the past and the present are not merely adjacent to each other in the shot but, through the identical tortilla basket continuing to appear without a break in both time-frames, past and present are momentarily one and the same.

Hitchcock uses more psychologised versions of this strategy in both *Vertigo* (1958) and *Marnie* (1964) when the same characters (not different ones or younger versions of the same ones, as in the example from Sayles) appear to inhabit discontinuous times and places within the continuity of a single shot. In the *Vertigo* example, Scottie (James Stewart) kisses Judy (Kim Novak) in her hotel room right after the completion of her transformation into the spitting image of Madeleine, the woman he has loved and apparently lost. Suddenly he finds himself back in the stable where he had kissed Madeleine (in one sense played by Kim Novak again, but, in another by Judy: that is, by Novak-as-Judy) earlier in the film. However, as with some of our other examples, it is difficult to find words to describe accurately what is happening both in narrative and in cinematic terms. Dan Auiler (1998: 119) explains the complicated techniques used in the shot,

FIGURE 17 *Scottie bewildered*

a combination of process footage from the two separate locations and the actors themselves on a turntable:

> The footage film in San Juan Bautista faded into a slow pan of Judy's hotel room to make the final process shot that was projected behind Stewart and Novak; the background resolved into a solid neon green as the shot ended. The impression thus created was that the camera was moving full circle around the lovers, when in reality it was the rear-projection image and the actors who were turning.

The distinction between diegetic and non-diegetic movement within the shot is blurred in two ways: first, there is perceptual uncertainty, as Auiler's words suggest (since the camera movement which we think is taking place is an illusion), and second, even if we know that the actors are on a moving turntable, it is a matter of considerable conceptual uncertainty whether this movement is diegetic or not. Put slightly differently, given that the actors are physically moving on the set, does it follow that their characters are moving in the narrative world?

What we have is not precisely a flashback, since Scottie looks wonder-ingly at the surrounding stable from what seems to be a vantage point out-side its space and time, yet he remains nonetheless immersed within the scene. A flashback would have transported the narrative past intact into the framing cinematic present, with all the characters within the flashback una-ware of being shown to us out of sequence. There are difficulties in know-ing precisely how to word this. Do flashbacks ever represent a movement back into the past (although surely not in the literal time-travelling sense)? Or are they always more accurately described as bringing past moments forward into the present (either as internal diegetic memories or as non-diegetic quotations)? My inclination is towards the latter formulation, since the present provides the outermost framing structure of most flashback sequences and thus has ontological primacy.

In any case, Scottie is bewildered by what appears to be his literal physi-cal transportation – as his present self – out of the present time and space in which he thought he was located (in the hotel room), so that the scene does not come across as a flashback, nor as an effect fully determined by an inner fantasy which swamps his consciousness. Instead, his partial awareness that something is amiss may reveal a glimmer of awareness that he is in a film whose world is being manipulated from elsewhere. His awareness of a breakdown in the narrative world's logic produces an effect very different from what would have resulted had Hitchcock dissolved to Scottie back in the stable as he was then, unaware of being simultaneously in another time and space. The diegetic events we see in this scene are inextricably enmeshed in their non-diegetic mode of presentation, so that it seems to be impossible to say what is happening within the narrative world – even at the level of bare description – without referring to the cin-ematic rhetoric that Hitchcock employs. What Scottie thinks is happening (lacking, as he does, any clear access to, and understanding of, this rheto-ric) is anyone's guess. One could almost claim that Hitchcock's cinematic strategies here take Scottie to the brink of madness as much as the more purely diegetic event of Madeleine's death (or what Scottie took to be the death of a woman whom he took to be Madeleine) had done.

This example is further complicated by the fact that Scottie's world is being manipulated not just by Hitchcock but by Gavin Elster (Tom Helmore) and his duplicitous behind-the-scenes stage management as well, through which he plans to convince Scottie that Judy-as-Madeleine is Elster's actual wife Madeleine and that her death is a suicide and not a murder. In Elster's 'production' too there are both diegetic and non-diegetic elements, so what we have is a layering of one diegetic/non-diegetic structure (Hitchcock's) upon another (Elster's). This layering is also a factor in the way we may think about the major characters in the film and their relationship to the stars who play them. Thus, if the enacted version of Madeleine (within the terms of Elster's schema) is really Judy, then Judy (within the terms of Hitchcock's film) is really Kim Novak, thereby complicating a process which is implicit in all dramatic enactments where the actor's non-diegetic body co-exists with the diegetic body of the character she plays. As George M. Wilson (1986: 141) puts it, discussing two of Dietrich's films with von Sternberg:

> In both films, the narration moves back and forth between a focus upon the character Dietrich portrays and an alternative focus on Dietrich herself – the real woman on a sound stage playing with her role. In *North by Northwest*, we discovered a variation on this ploy.

So, although characters may be given histories and psychologies of their own which locate them within the narrative world, their bodies are necessarily on loan from the world outside the film, their physical presence both diegetic and non-diegetic at the same time, although Wilson goes on to caution that:

> our troubles about film narration are compounded by the absence of clear criteria for sorting out what belongs to a film's narrative, on the one hand, and to the narration, on the other. In the King Vidor version of *War and Peace*, Henry Fonda, speaking in his familiar,

distinctive Midwestern accent, plays the part of Pierre, but this aspect of his performance does not signify that Pierre speaks with such an accent or some Russian analogue to it.

If Scottie, while subject to Elster's scenario, occupies a spectatorial position analogous to our own with respect to Hitchcock's film, nonetheless we are much more aware of watching a film than Scottie is of watching Elster's production. Whereas we know throughout that Novak-as-actress is playing the part of Judy, Scottie's conscious awareness (and, indeed, our own) that Judy is a kind of actress playing the part of Madeleine under Elster's direction is delayed until well into the film.

Before we leave *Vertigo*, it may be relevant to mention a further example of diegetic/non-diegetic slippage in the odd transition which occurs at the end of Scottie's meeting with Elster at the latter's club, the scene ending as Scottie remarks, 'Boy, I need this,' and downs a drink. At this point, the image fades so quickly to black that, unless the film is advanced a frame at a time, it looks for all the world like a cut. Although fades are non-diegetic devices, cuts are conventionally understood as instantaneous transitions between different bits of the narrative world, so the blackness of the screen after the not quite instantaneous fade seems almost to constitute a blackness in the film's narrative world itself, a momentary annihilation or rupture of its fabric. Madeleine's account of her dream to Scottie ('I was alone in the dark'), as well as the image of the open, gaping grave in Scottie's dream, provide more straightforwardly diegetic equivalents of this effect and reinforce the deathly associations of the ambiguous edit at the club with its suggestion that what we are confronting is the possibility of the obliteration or death of the narrative world altogether. One might mention, in passing, Hitchcock's technique of disguising the edits, as in *Rope* (1948), so that the camera's movement onto a dark object within the narrative world at the end of the long takes misrepresents as diegetic the non-diegetic transitions between shots, the blackness at these junctures providing yet another example of ontological duality, that is, an example of two separate realms of existence layered one upon the other.

Hitchcock's fondness for expressionist devices throughout his work – where internal psychological states are externalised and expressed in cinematic form – provides numerous further instances where diegetic and non-diegetic aspects of a film are difficult to disentangle, for example the use of red in *Marnie*, which washes over the narrative world whenever Marnie panics. Although the colour is certainly not part of the external diegetic world, we may wish to claim that it 'has its origin inside a character's mind,' which are Buckland's words for what he calls the internal diegetic (as quoted earlier). However, what we presume to exist in Marnie's mind is a feeling, not a colour. So the red seems there for us, in order to indicate something quite separate which Marnie is experiencing (or perhaps to make us experience a comparable panic, in our case at the apparent rupture of the narrative world as the redness 'bleeds' across it from this putative 'wound'), rather like the way that soundtrack music may be used to indicate a character's state of mind or to put us in a sympathetic mood, although the red seems more directly triggered by narrative events or states than soundtrack music does.

An even more difficult example to pin down is the moment in Hitchcock's *The Wrong Man* (1956) when Manny Balestrero (Henry Fonda) is seated alone and bewildered in the prison cell where he has been wrongfully incarcerated, and the view of him in his cell which we face head-on begins to spin in a clockwise direction with Manny at its centre before fading to black. It is not the room itself which spins, but rather the image as a whole. Nonetheless it is unclear whether this spinning image is for our benefit alone as an indication of Manny's general disorientation (as the red washes express Marnie's panic for us even if she does not see red herself) or whether it is to be taken as a literal depiction of Manny's psychological state. Instead of being a clear case of either the internal diegetic or the non-diegetic, these red washes seem to constitute an interface between the space of the narrative world and the space we inhabit as viewers, a space neither wholly within the diegesis nor wholly outside it.

Such an imaginary domain is powerfully activated in Hitchcock's films, as these various examples have suggested, although we have also seen how such things as musical numbers, flashbacks, and voice-over narration addressed by a character to the viewer are common generic devices (in the musical and film noir, respectively) which expand the reach of this shared domain where characters are lifted out of their more usual positions within the narrative world to imaginatively inhabit an ontological borderland somewhere between their diegetic world and ours. However, our position as spectators is not symmetrically balanced with the characters' positions within the narrative world as if the borderland marked the interface of two spaces of equal ontological weight. Because we are located at the outer layer of the overall structure, physically grounded in the non-diegetic world and looking in, we have a much greater awareness than the characters can ever have, embedded as they are in a world which makes them largely blind to our own world outside it and only occasionally and dimly aware of their fixture within the larger structure. Thus they may sing to a music they cannot logically hear, be assailed by images lobbed at them from a place beyond their ability to see, inhabit bodies not fully their own, and address spectators they can barely imagine. The oddity of these possibilities, although only rarely brought explicitly to our attention, may nevertheless contribute to the fascination of many Hollywood films and the strange combination they so often present of illogical dreamscape and believable world.

Virtual and real

What has been thus far explored by no means encompasses all the ways in which spectators and characters may interact: no mention has been made of our emotional or moral involvement with the narrative world, which is usually discussed in terms of such concepts as 'identification' or 'engagement'. Instead we are concentrating on the ways and the extent to which spectators and characters may look each other's way and offer some acknowledgement – however impaired their vision – both of one another's spatial separateness and of some common ground between them. At this point it is necessary to consider the screen itself – the flat rectangular meeting-place between the narrative world and our own location at its outer rim – since it is what both characters and spectators come up against as the limiting boundary of their respective worlds.

Although we have noted the importance of camera movement and off-screen space in producing a sense of the three-dimensionality of the narrative world, it is still a world we can only see through the two-dimensionality of the screen. Thus, if we construe the screen as a transparent plane of rectangular shape between us and the narrative world, then even if we were to watch a film whose camera was continually circling around within the spaces of the narrative world, it would be as if our imaginary screen were turning on its axis while moving through space like a mobile revolving door, with us condemned to remain forever on the opposite side from the action. Another way of putting this is that we do not generally imagine the action of a film to be going on behind us, so completely are we orientated to the narrative world 'out there' in front of us, just as that world, from its own perspective, faces and is orientated across the screen to us. The characters, of course, are aware of the space behind them: their difficulties are in being in a narrative world which is generally orientated towards the front of the screen while having no clear sense of our presence beyond it, although the camera's movement within that world allows their orientation towards the screen to be preserved without their necessarily becoming aware of this.

Sound may create an illusion of an offscreen space in which, in some sense, we are immersed – what Mary Ann Doane calls 'the sonorous envelope provided by the theatrical space' (1985: 171) – although Christian Metz points out that the relationship between sound and screen is far from straightforward:

> In a film a sound is considered 'off' (literally off the screen) when in fact it is the sound's source that is off the screen ... We tend to forget that a sound in itself is never 'off': either it is audible or it doesn't exist. When it exists, it could not possibly be situated within the interior of the rectangle or outside of it, since the nature of sounds is to diffuse themselves more or less into the entire surrounding space: sound is simultaneously 'in' the screen, in front, behind, around, and throughout the entire movie theatre (1985: 157–8).

The effect of this seems to me to be very different in films from the way that radio's sounds, say, wrap an imaginary world around us, since radio listeners are not orientated in space in a comparable way, with the radio itself acting as a similar sort of reference point to the screen. Although on a purely physical level, sounds in both film and radio are certainly perceived as coming from particular locations in space, we are concerned more with our imaginative locations within their respective narrative worlds, which transcend the directional sources of their sounds. Examining one's own experience may suggest that the illusion of space created by a radio drama is easier to insert oneself within (particularly if one closes one's eyes), precisely because the radio medium lacks film's strong visual sense of ontological separation between its world and ours, produced by the screen, which would tend to override any enveloping effects produced by sound alone.

However, our sense of spatial exclusion from a film's narrative world – no matter how much visual and aural access to it we may have – does not appear to result from any over-awareness of our own bodies and the physical space in which we are actually sitting as we watch. If I have no sense of a portion of the narrative world behind me, then neither am I unduly conscious of any other space behind me outside of the film, at least to the extent that I am absorbed in the film: noisy popcorn eaters in the row behind me may provide a momentary distraction, but generally my awareness is orientated only towards what is in front of me in the narrative world. My experience is of being right at that border between the screen and the world beyond it, with little awareness of the space between my eyes and the screen (thus, my awareness of viewers in the rows in front of me is also generally suppressed). In spatial terms a film has the capacity to draw us right up to the screen, but no further. Even when the camera leads us into the depths of the narrative world, through a forward tracking shot, it is still as if we bear the rectangular screen before us, rather than our crossing through it to enter that world, with its earlier foreground spaces now closing around us at our back as we proceed. Indeed, it would be just as accurate, in purely visual terms, to describe such shots in terms of the background moving forward towards the screen to meet us as it would be to

FIGURE 18 *Mirror shot of Alvah smoking*

describe them in terms of us moving into the depths of the narrative world, and this descriptive ambiguity provides a visual analogue to the temporal ambiguities noted earlier in descriptions of flashbacks as, alternatively, the movements of characters and viewers from the present into the past or the bringing forward of past moments into the present. Such a description of forward movement towards the viewer is even more compelling when an illusion of offscreen space is created in front of the screen (on our side of it), where the effect is as if a virtual version of the screen itself were to move towards us to encompass such offscreen portions of the narrative world, rather than to place these offscreen spaces behind us.

To give a more specific instance, the technique of implying offscreen space in front of the screen through the use of onscreen mirrors which reflect parts of the offscreen narrative world, rather than reflecting us within the mirrors as we look, underscores our own invisibility rather than creating an illusion of bits of the narrative world existing behind us, and this reinforces in a very blatant way the non-corporeal nature of our experience of viewing narrative films more generally. A number of examples may be found of this in Fritz Lang's *Cloak and Dagger* (1946), for instance when we see Gina (Lily Palmer) brushing her hair in the foreground, her back to us as she looks in a mirror, with not only Gina reflected in the mirror, but also Alvah Jasper (Gary Cooper) smoking a cigarette behind her, although he appears only as a reflection. Indeed, we saw a similar example in the discussion of *Advise and Consent* when Brig's wife was offscreen yet appeared behind him in the bathroom mirror, although the mirror in the Lang example is somewhat less angled and more fully facing on to the spectator (though not completely), so that our own invisibility is, perhaps, more marked.

It is worth asking ourselves, in relation to the *Cloak and Dagger* example, where exactly we imagine Alvah to be standing relative to ourselves. Is it not the case that we take him to be in front of us and slightly to the right, somewhere between ourselves and the screen, and do we not find ourselves pulling back in our imaginations from the screen which is normally coextensive with our visual field in order to 'make room' for an extended 'virtual' portion of this visual field as implied by what we see in the mirror? Once again, it is difficult to find words to capture our experience with precision, although something decidedly odd seems to be going on. The oddity is even stronger when, later in the scene, it is Gina who is visible only in the mirror as she sits on the bed, and it is Alvah who stands to the right of the mirror looking at her offscreen. As we see her in the mirror looking back at him, his gaze and hers in the mirror are completely unaligned. The image which we nonetheless unambiguously read as a meeting of their gazes depends on her offscreen presence between the screen and us at a point precisely determined by the direction of his gaze, and therefore easy to pinpoint as being in front of us, not behind.

Our experience in watching films is not so much a matter of seeing from a specific position (as it is when watching live theatre, where one's physical location in the audience determines viewpoint much more fully, and moving to another seat can provide a significantly better view), but instead it is as if we were lifted out of our bodies to inhabit a sort of virtual space

FIGURE 19 *Mirror shot of Gina on the bed*

of pure and disembodied vision. This suggests that our imaginary location is at the interface provided between the narrative world and the real world outside it either by the screen itself or, in the case of a mirror reflecting offscreen space in front of the screen, by a kind of virtual screen which is projected outward towards us by this technique. We remain, in either instance, without any clear sense of a portion of the narrative world behind our backs, not even the minimal sense required to insert us within this world rather than at its outer rim. Of course, we know that the onscreen world – insofar as we take it as 'real' – extends indefinitely in all directions and does not stop where our visual field begins. Nevertheless, it feels at any given moment as if it is all before us.

This demonstrates an ambiguity comparable to those presented from the characters' points of view in the previous section where, at times, they inhabit what was described as an ontological borderland between diegetic and non-diegetic spaces and logical schemas. We too are neither within nor outside of the narrative world as we watch, with neither a clear-cut impression of its spaces extending all around us nor a dominating awareness of our real location in the world outside the film. When I examine my own experience of watching a film, it feels to me as though I am positioned at the boundary produced by the screen (or by the extended virtual screen), not as myself, but, rather, as a disembodied viewer, unreflected in mirrors, unseen by characters within the film, and taken out of my real body in the film theatre or in my easy chair at home. If a film's characters have two bodies – their own and those of the actors who portray them – then we, in contrast, would appear to have none.

Such disembodiment is particularly relevant to point-of-view shots where we are positioned exactly where one or another character is, yet without necessarily forfeiting a sense of separateness and even of alienation from them (as is the case in many horror films, for example, which use this technique to give us access to the point of view of a monster not in order to encourage identification with such monsters but in order to arouse our anxiety towards other characters whom they are stalking and to whom they pose a threat). Even though we look through such characters' eyes, we are somehow still able to differentiate ourselves from them a little and to open up an imaginary space between us and them without relinquishing this access to their visual field. It is precisely the fact that we watch films as if we are disembodied which makes this possible. As Terence Penelhum remarks in the context of a discussion about the logical possibility of disembodied perception:

> Someone might say: to give a disembodied person these capacities you are giving him a body back surreptitiously. This is not so. If he had his body back he would see it again; and he does not ... And if he had his body back, it would fill the space that other objects occupy, and it does not (1970: 35).

Such point-of-view shots seem fundamentally different in kind from certain types of foreground shots of the back of a character's head when the

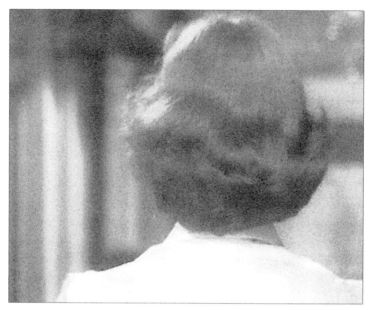

FIGURE 20 *Back of head shot of Eva*

character is ostentatiously turned away from us, rather than merely from another character in the narrative world. Although it may appear as if point-of-view shots are logical extensions of such back-of-the-head shots, the limiting case in a continuum whereby characters move further and further back towards the camera until they are completely offscreen, it seems that, once characters back out of the onscreen portion of the narrative world (except for those cases where they remain reflected in an onscreen mirror), something quite different is going on from when they remain visible from behind on the screen. Hitchcock uses back-of-the-head shots in *Stage Fright* and *Vertigo* when Eve and Judy respectively are seen in the fore-ground from behind. In each case the moment is associated with duplicity on the character's part and the possibility of a well-constructed façade falling apart, the moment of crisis clearly signalled to us by the rhetorical device. In Eve's case, she arrives home late for tea with a detective she had invited round in order to find out more about a murder case he is

115

investigating, in which a man she likes has been implicated, misleading the detective into believing her romantic interest is in him. Suddenly her father, who is in on her schemings and whom she had not noticed in the room, begins to speak, and Hitchcock cuts to the back of Eve's head which dominates the frame and blocks our view. The shot emphasises Eve's shiftiness and the danger that she may be found out, as she tries to collect herself not just for the detective but for the camera and us. Our inability to see either Eve's face or the rest of the room beyond her may even contribute to our feeling excluded or betrayed, when not just Eve but the narrative world itself appears to avert its face.

Whereas we are aware of Eve's designs from the start, in the example from *Vertigo* we do not yet know that Judy and Madeleine are one and the same. Having got Judy to agree to have dinner with him later that night, Scottie leaves her room, and the camera moves left onto the back of Judy's head in the foreground of the frame as she watches him go. After she turns towards us, the lighting changes as the shot dissolves to a flashback version of what really happened, and we discover the extent of her betrayal. However, although the flashback and her subsequent letter to Scottie make all this explicit, the back-of-the-head shot has alerted us to her duplicity even sooner. Both these examples suggest that when a character is unable to face the camera and receive our gaze, it may be because her identity is momentarily so unstable that she needs time to recompose and reconstitute herself so that the narrative can resume. So fundamental is our assumption that the narrative world will face our way that in those rare moments when it appears to turn away from us, its own stability appears under threat.

This chapter is much more speculative than the previous three, and the length of the present book does not permit a more thorough exploration of these issues. What I hope to have done is to have opened the way for further consideration of spectators' relationships to films in terms of space. American films made within the studio system seem particularly prone to oddities and ambiguities of the sorts mentioned, with characters slipping in and out of the diegetic realm, and spectators poised in a condition of virtual disembodiment at the interface between the narrative world and the real physical world on our side of the screen. We have seen that the sense of ontological ambiguity in such films contributes to their combination of dreamy elusiveness and narrative accessibility. It is a central aspect of their enduring fascination.

Suggestions for further reading

Most discussions of diegetic and non-diegetic aspects of films are focused on music, like many of the texts cited above (for example Doane (1985); Laing (2000); Metz (1985)), while Perkins (2000) provides an account of Letter from an Unknown Woman which looks at the lapses in conventional narrative logic in its flashback structure. In terms of the relationship between viewers and onscreen space, Sallitt (1980) argues that point-of-view shots in Hitchcock's films function to relate us directly to the narrative worlds of these films, rather than to align us with specific characters within them, and Smith (2000) provides a useful counter-argument to some of his claims.

CONCLUSION

This book has attributed particular importance to the close analysis of individual films as potential sites of complex meanings. The process of reading Hollywood films has been represented here as an inherently democratic one, and the purpose of presenting others with one's own particular insights about a film and its mechanisms is to return them to the film to see for themselves. Given a certain baseline familiarity with American culture and its products, anyone who has eyes to see and ears to hear can explore the ways that a Hollywood film works upon us as audience. The 'data' for such observations are accessible to all. Although practice and the examples of others will be of the greatest importance in helping us to develop skills of close observation and analysis for ourselves, I have suggested a number of questions about significant spaces in Hollywood films and the meanings embedded within them as a first step in this direction. However, there remain many more questions which can be asked, and other accounts of the reading process may offer alternative routes in.

The democratic way of construing this methodology which makes room for a multitude of readings of a given film is incompatible with any notion of a definitive version, particularly one vested in the authority of an 'expert' reader. Nevertheless, some analyses of individual films are clearly more useful than others in opening up and developing our understanding of important aspects of the films (just as films themselves may vary in the nature and quality of the experience they provide). It is a further tenet of this book that close readings have the potential to be far from trivial and may lead us to considerations of substantial depth and sophistication for an understanding not only of specific films but of such things as our culture and our location within it.

In Chapter 1 we saw how the significance of various spaces within *My Darling Clementine* and *Party Girl* assumes and depends upon the viewer's familiarity with a combination of historical facts and cultural myths (about the settlement of the West and the urbanising of modern America) which imbue geographical and architectural settings and structures with meanings from a larger social and generic context. Further, the films gain depth and complexity from the specific ways that issues such as gender are mapped across their narrative worlds, affecting the ways their characters inhabit space and time. In Chapter 2, our exploration of the theme of scandal in small-town melodramas uncovered the way that such films may give us sympathetic access to a character's 'backstage' moments, and that the characters who have most to gain are those whose public performances are most tightly monitored and controlled. It is not possible to understand such films as these, even at the level of plot, without being aware of the cultural significance of racial and sexual differences. To take note of slaves and unfaithful wives, for example, while simultaneously investigating a film's strategies for deploying our sympathies, is to invoke social structures and political positions from the world outside the film. Similarly, in Chapter 3, our close reading of the cinematic treatment of space in *Advise and Consent* revealed parallels between women and homosexual men who equally risk being pushed to the sidelines of power within the institutions of marriage and government in a narrative world not so very different from our own. Thus, any stark opposition between text and context is a false one. It turns out to be impossible to talk about a film – or even to experience it in a meaningful way – without drawing upon broader cultural knowledge and ideological concerns, unless we reduce the film to little more than a shifting pattern of non-representational shapes and sounds. The preoccupations of Chapter 4 are more philosophical and less obviously grounded in social concerns, but they too draw upon a context larger than themselves: the context of the viewing experience and a film's relationship to its audience.

This book resists canonising films (or critical accounts) in any absolute way, although certain sorts of judgements about the qualities of a given film or reading are nonetheless hard to avoid. Thus, a film may be deemed particularly intelligent and effective in its exposure of the pain involved in being black in a racist world (e.g. *Mandingo*; *Imitation of Life*) or female in a sexist world (e.g. *My Darling Clementine*; *All I Desire*) or even in being white and male in a repressive world which spares no one with its harsh demands (e.g. *Party Girl*). Readings which alert us to such things and help us to understand the social mechanisms which bring them about may be worthwhile for those who seek social change and who see a film's world as having certain affinities with our own. Acknowledging the positive qualities which we can ascribe to particular films and close readings – positive, that is, not in any absolute way, but relative to a shared set of values and aspirations between them and us – is clearly a matter of evaluation, but surely no more so than the way that any cultural product or critical account which offers itself to the world does so with an implicit assertion of its own value, however that may be defined. Thus, theorists or critics who reject textual analysis because it is seen to be evaluative are themselves evaluating such an approach and finding it to be qualitatively inferior to their own.

I have argued that the criticisms which are sometimes levelled against textual analysis – the assertions that such a methodology is necessarily élitist or trivial or that it elevates particular film texts while ignoring broader contexts – are caricatures of a process which has the potential to offer as much depth of insight as any other. As long as such accounts help us to understand aspects of a film that matter to us, then such accounts will also matter. It is not the methodology itself, but the uses to which it is put that determine its value.

FILMOGRAPHY

Advise and Consent (Otto Preminger, 1962, US)
All I Desire (Douglas Sirk, 1953, US)
All That Heaven Allows (Douglas Sirk, 1956, US)
The Bigamist (Ida Lupino, 1953, US)
Brigadoon (Vincente Minnelli, 1954, US)
Cloak and Dagger (Fritz Lang, 1946, US)
Home From the Hill (Vincente Minnelli, 1960, US)
Imitation of Life (Douglas Sirk, 1958, US)
It's a Wonderful Life (Frank Capra, 1946, US)
Kings Row (Sam Wood, 1942, US)
Letter From an Unknown Woman (Max Ophuls, 1948, US)
Lone Star (John Sayles, 1996, US)
Mandingo (Richard Fleischer, 1975, US)
Marnie (Alfred Hitchcock, 1964, US)
Meet Me in St Louis (Vincente Minnelli, 1944, US)
My Darling Clementine (John Ford, 1946, US)
Party Girl (Nicholas Ray, 1958, US)
Rebecca (Alfred Hitchcock, 1940, US)
Rebel Without a Cause (Nicholas Ray, 1955, US)
Rope (Alfred Hitchcock, 1948, US)
Some Came Running (Vincente Minnelli, 1958, US)
Stage Fright (Alfred Hitchcock, 1950, US)
Touch of Evil (Orson Welles, 1958, US)
Vertigo (Alfred Hitchcock, 1958, US)
Woman in the Window (Fritz Lang, 1944, US)
Written on the Wind (Douglas Sirk, 1956, US)
The Wrong Man (Alfred Hitchcock, 1956, US)

BIBLIOGRAPHY

The bibliography lists works cited in the text and is also designed to point to useful further read-ing. The annotated list of 'essential reading' highlights works considered to be of particular impor-tance to contemporary understandings of topics most central to this book, such as aspects of space, meaning, narrative, point-of-view, and genre.

ESSENTIAL READING

Belton, J. (1992) *Widescreen Cinema*. Massachusetts and London: Harvard University Press.
 An interesting examination of the changing shape of the cinema screen in the 1950s, combin-ing historical and technical material with speculations on the implications for film meaning and spectatorship.

Bordwell, D., J. Staiger & K. Thompson (eds) (1985) *The Classical Hollywood Cinema: Film Style & Mode of Production to 1960*. London, Melbourne and Henley: Routledge & Kegan Paul.
 This ambitious empirical study is based on a sample of American feature films from 1915 to 1960 and provides a descriptive account of the norms of studio film-making throughout this period.

Maltby, R. & I. Craven (eds) (1995) *Hollywood Cinema*. Oxford: Blackwell.
 A wide-ranging introduction to Hollywood cinema with sections on entertainment, genre, industry, technology, space, performance, time, narrative, politics and criticism.

Marx, L. (1964) *The Machine in the Garden: Technology and the Pastoral Ideal in America*. Oxford, London and New York: Oxford University Press.
 Investigates the enduring hold upon the American imagination of the concept of the pastoral as an ideal cultivated landscape between primitive nature and the corruptions of the social world.

Neale, S. (2000) *Genre and Hollywood*. London and New York: Routledge.
  A scholarly introduction to Hollywood genres and genre theory with an extensive bibliography and frame of reference.

Perkins, V. F. (1972) *Film as Film: Understanding and Judging Movies*. Harmondsworth: Penguin.
  A clear and intelligent text from a highly respected critic in the mise-en-scène tradition which explores the issues at stake in analysing and evaluating films.

—— (1990)'Must We Say What They Mean?: Film Criticism and Interpretation', *Movie*, 34/35, 1–6.
  A more recent account from Perkins which develops his philosophical concerns with meaning and interpretation while differentiating his position from that of David Bordwell (1989) and setting out the terms of the debate.

Smith, H. N. (1950) *Virgin Land: The American West as Symbol and Myth*. Cambridge, Massachusetts and London: Harvard University Press.
  This influential book is indispensable for understanding the significance of the American landscape and its relationship to popular culture.

Thomas, D. (2000) *Beyond Genre: Melodrama, Comedy and Romance in Hollywood Films*. London and Moffat: Cameron & Hollis.
  A mapping of American films in terms of broad melodramatic, comedic and romantic categories, which pays particular attention to the way space is structured in films of each type.

Wertheim, M. (1999) *The Pearly Gates of Cyberspace: A History of Space From Dante to the Internet*. London: Virago Press.
  An accessible discussion of various frameworks – philosophical, scientific, literary and artistic – for understanding space in different historical periods.

White, M. and L. White (1977) *The Intellectual versus the City: from Thomas Jefferson to Frank Lloyd Wright*. Oxford, London and New York: Oxford University Press.
  A useful account of attitudes to the city within American culture and their historical underpinnings.

Wilson, G. M. (1986) *Narration in Light: Studies in Cinematic Point of View*. Baltimore and London: Johns Hopkins University Press.
  A difficult but immensely rewarding book which alternates theoretical explorations of aspects of point of view with detailed accounts of particular American films.

SECONDARY READING

Andrew, G. (1991) *The Films of Nicholas Ray*. London: Letts.

Auiler, D. (1998) *Vertigo: The Making of a Hitchcock Classic*. New York: St. Martin's Press.

Bordwell, D. (1989) *Making Meaning: Inference and Rhetoric in the Interpretation of Cinema*. Massachusetts and London: Harvard University Press.

Britton, A. (1976) 'Mandingo', *Movie*, 22, 1–22.

Brown, R. S. (1994) *Overtones and Undertones: Reading Film Music*. Berkeley and London: University of California Press.

Buckland, W. (1998) *Teach Yourself Film Studies*. London: Hodder & Stoughton.

Buscombe, E. and R. E. Pearson (eds) (1998) *Back in the Saddle Again: New Essays on the Western*. London: BFI.

Cameron, I. (ed.) (1992) *The Movie Book of Film Noir*. London: Studio Vista.

Cameron, I. and D. Pye (eds) (1996) *The Movie Book of the Western*. London: Studio Vista.

Cavell, S. (1981) *Pursuits of Happiness: The Hollywood Comedy of Remarriage*. Massachusetts and London: Harvard University Press.

—— (1996) *Contesting Tears: The Hollywood Melodrama of the Unknown Woman*. Chicago and London: University of Chicago Press.

Cook, P. and M. Bernink (eds) (1999) *The Cinema Book*. London: BFI.

Davis, R. L. (1995) *John Ford: Hollywood's Old Master*. Norman and London: University of Oklahoma Press.

Doane, M. A. (1985) 'The Voice in the Cinema: The Articulation of Body and Space', in E. Weis and J. Belton (eds) *Film Sound: Theory and Practice*. New York: Columbia University Press, 162–76.

Feuer, J. (1982) *The Hollywood Musical*. London and Basingstoke: Macmillan.

Gallafent, E. (1996) 'Four Tombstones 1946–1994', in I. Cameron and D. Pye (eds) *The Movie Book of the Western*. London: Studio Vista, 302–11.

Gledhill, C. (ed.) (1987) *Home is where the Heart Is: Studies in Melodrama and the Woman's Film*. London: BFI.

Gledhill, C. and L. Williams (eds) (2000) *Reinventing Film Studies*. London: Arnold.

Goffman, E. (1974) *Frame Analysis: An Essay on the Organisation of Experience*. Harmondsworth: Penguin.

Grant, B. K. (1995) *Film Genre Reader II*. Austin: University of Texas Press.

Hayward, S. (1996) *Key Concepts in Cinema Studies*. London and New York: Routledge.

Hirsch, F. (1981) *The Dark Side of the Screen: Film Noir*. New York: Da Capo Press.

Kaplan, E. A. (ed.) (1998) *Women in Film Noir*. London: BFI.

Karnick, K. B. and H. Jenkins (eds) (1995) *Classical Hollywood Comedy*. New York and London: Routledge.

Krutnik, F. (1991) *In a Lonely Street: Film Noir, Genre and Masculinity*. London: Routledge.

Laing, H. (2000) 'Emotion By Numbers: Music, Song and the Musical', in B. Marshall & R. Stilwell (eds) *Musicals: Hollywood and Beyond*. Exeter and Portland: Intellect Books, 5–13.

McBride, J. and M. Wilmington (1974) *John Ford*. London: Secker & Warburg.

Metz, C. (1985) 'Aural Objects', in E. Weis and J. Belton (eds) *Film Sound: Theory and Practice*. New York: Columbia University Press, 154–61.

Monaco, J. (1977) *How to Read a Film: the Art, Technology, Language, History, and Theory of Film and Media*. Oxford and New York: Oxford University Press.

Neale, S. and F. Krutnik (1990) *Popular Film and Television Comedy*. London and New York: Routledge.

Penelhum, T. (1970) *Survival and Disembodied Existence*. London: Routledge & Kegan Paul.

Perkins, V. F. (2000) 'Same Tune Again! Repetition and Framing in Letter from an Unknown Woman', *CineAction*, 52, 40–8.

Pye, D. (2000) 'Movies and Point of View', *Movie*, 36, 2–34.

Sallitt, D. (1980) 'Point of View and "Intrarealism"', *Wide Angle*, 4, 1, 38–43.

Smith, S. (2000) *Hitchcock: Suspense, Humour and Tone*. London: BFI.

Thomas, D. (1992a) 'How Hollywood Deals with the Deviant Male', in I. Cameron (ed.) *The Movie Book of Film Noir*. London: Studio Vista, 59–70.

—— (1992b) 'Psychoanalysis and Film Noir', in Cameron (ed.) *The Movie Book of Film Noir*. London: Studio Vista, 71–87.

Thompson, K. (1999) *Storytelling in the New Hollywood: Understanding Classical Narrative Technique*. Massachusetts and London: Harvard University Press.

Weis, E. and J. Belton (eds) (1985) *Film Sound: Theory and Practice*. New York: Columbia University Press.

Wood, M. (1975) *America in the Movies or, 'Santa Maria, It Had Slipped My Mind!'*. London: Secker & Warburg.

Wood, R. (1962) 'Attitudes in *Advise and Consent*', *Movie*, 4, 14–17.

—— (1977) 'Ideology, Genre, Auteur', *Film Comment*, 13, 1, 46–51.

THE SHORT CUTS SERIES

A comprehensive library of introductory texts covering the full spectrum of Film Studies, specifically designed for building an individually styled library for all students and enthusiasts of cinema and popular culture.

"This series is tailor-made for a modular approach to film studies ... an indispensable tool for both lecturers and students"

01 THE HORROR GENRE
FROM BEELZEBUB TO BLAIR WITCH
Paul Wells

The inaugral book in the Short Cuts series is a comprehensive introduction to the history and key themes of the horror genre. The main issues and debates raised by horror, and the approaches and theories that have been applied to horror texts are all addressed. In charting the evolution of the horror film in social and cultural context, Paul Wells explores how it has reflected and commented upon particular historical periods, and asks how it may respond to the new millennium by citing recent innovations in the genre's development, such as the 'urban myth' narrative underpinning *Candyman* and *The Blair Witch Project*.

"An informed and highly readable account that is theoretically broad, benefiting from a wide range of cinematic examples."

1-903364-00-0   144 pp.

02 THE STAR SYSTEM
HOLLYWOOD'S PRODUCTION OF POPULAR IDENTITIES
Paul McDonald

The Star System looks at the development and changing organization of the star system in the American film industry. Tracing the popularity of star performers from the early 'cinema of attractions' to the internet universe, Paul McDonald explores the ways in which Hollywood has made and sold its stars. Through focusing on particular historical periods, the key conditions influencing the star system in silent cinema, the studio era and the New Hollywood are discussed and illustrated by cases studies of Mary Pickford, Bette Davis, James Cagney, Julia Roberts, Tom Cruise, and Will Smith.

"A very good introduction to the topic filling an existing gap in the needs of researchers and students of the subject."
Roberta Pearson, University of Wales, Cardiff

1-903364-02-7   144 pp.

03 SCIENCE FICTION CINEMA
FROM OUTERSPACE TO CYBERSPACE
Geoff King and Tanya Krzywinska

Science Fiction Cinema charts the dimensions of one of the most popular film genres. From lurid comic-book blockbusters to dark dystopian visions, science fiction is seen as both a powerful cultural barometer of our times and the product of particular industrial and commercial frameworks. The authors outline the major themes of the genre, from representations of the mad scientist and computer hacker to the relationship between science fiction and postmodernism, exploring issues such as the meaning of special effects and the influence of science fiction cinema on the entertainment media of the digital age.

"The best overview of English-language science fiction cinema published to date... thorough, clearly written and full of excellent examples. Highly recommended."
Steve Neale, Sheffield Hallam University

1-903364-03-5   144 pp.

04   EARLY SOVIET CINEMA
INNOVATION. IDEOLOGY AND PROPAGANDA.
David Gillespie

Early Soviet Cinema examines the aesthetics of Soviet cinema during its 'golden age' of the 1920s, against a background of cultural ferment and the construction of a new socialist society. Separate chapters are devoted to the work of Sergei Eisenstein, Lev Kuleshov, Vsevolod Pudovkin, Dziga Vertov and Alexander Dovzhenko. Other major directors are also discussed at length. David Gillespie places primary focus on the text, with analysis concentrating on the artistic qualities, rather than the political implications, of each film. The result is not only a discussion of each director's contribution to the 'golden age' and to world cinema, but also an exploration of their own distinctive poetics.

"An excellent book ... Lively and informative, it fills a significant gap and deserves to be on reading lists wherever courses on Soviet cinema are run."

Graham Roberts, University of Surrey

1-903364-04-3   128 pp.

06   DISASTER MOVIES
THE CINEMA OF CATASTROPHE
Stephen Keane

Disaster Movies provides a comprehensive introduction to the history and development of the disaster genre. The 1950s sci-fi B-movies to high concept 1990s 'millennial movies', Stephen Keane looks at the ways in which the representation of disaster and its aftermath are borne out of both contextual considerations and the increasing commercial demands of contemporary Hollywood. Through detailed analyses of such films as *Airport*, *The PoseidonAdventure*, *Independence Day* and *Titanic*, the book explores the continual reworking of this, to-date, undervalued genre.

"Providing detailed consideration of key movies within their social and cultural context, this concise introduction serves its purpose well and should prove a useful teaching tool."

Nick Roddick

1-903364-05-1   144 pp.

07   NEW CHINESE CINEMA
CHALLENGING REPRESENTATIONS
Sheila Cornelius

New Chinese Cinema examines the 'search for roots' films that emerged from China in the aftermath of the Cultural Revolution. Sheila Cornelius contextualises the films of the so-called 'Fifth Generation' directors who came to prominence in the 1980s and 1990s, such as Chen Kaige, Zhang Yimou and Tian Zhuangzhuan. Including close analysis of such pivotal films as *Farewell My Concubine*, *Raise the Red Lantern* and *The Blue Kite*, the book also examines the rise of contemporary 'Sixth Generation' underground directors whose themse embrace the disaffection of urban youth.

"Very thorough in its coverage of the historical and cultural background to New Chinese Cinema ... clearly written and appropriately targeted at an undergraduate audience."

Leon Hunt, Brunel University

1-903364-13-2   144 pp.

08   THE WESTERN GENRE
FROM LORDSBURG TO BIG WHISKEY
John Saunders

The Western Genre offers close readings of the definitive American film movement as represented by such leading exponents as John Ford, Howard Hawks and Sam Peckinpah. In his consideration of such iconic motifs as the Outlaw Hero and the Lone Rider, John Saunders traces the development of perennial aspects of the genre, its continuity and, importantly, its change. Representations of morality and masculinity are also foregrounded in consideration of the genre's major stars John Wayne and Clint Eastwood, and the book includes a number of detailed analyses of such landmark films as *Shane*, *Rio Bravo*, *The Wild Bunch* and *Unforgiven*.

"A clear exposition of the major thematic currents of the genre providing attentive and illuminating readings of major examples."

Ed Buscombe, editor of *The BFI Companion to the Western*

1-903364-12-4   144 pp.